MW01242201

PROUD TO BE PROUD

❋ *A MEMOIR:* ❋

The True Story of an American Family
From Slavery into the Twenty-First Century

MARY DILLINGHAM

authorHOUSE™

1663 LIBERTY DRIVE, SUITE 200
BLOOMINGTON, INDIANA 47403
(800) 839-8640
WWW.AUTHORHOUSE.COM

AuthorHouse™
1663 Liberty Drive, Suite 200
Bloomington, IN 47403
www.authorhouse.com
Phone: 1-800-839-8640

AuthorHouse™ UK Ltd.
500 Avebury Boulevard
Central Milton Keynes, MK9 2BE
www.authorhouse.co.uk
Phone: 08001974150

First published by AuthorHouse 2/27/2006

ISBN: 1-4208-8636-3 (sc)

Library of Congress Control Number: 2005908879

Printed in the United States of America
Bloomington, Indiana

This book is printed on acid-free paper.

*This book is dedicated to the memory of
My Parents, Rev. John and Pearl Martin*

and

*My Grandmother, Mamie Veal Burney
(also known as Mary Wright)*

Because of them, I am me.

FOREWORD

This book represents a portrait of America, as seen through the eyes and personal experiences of a now-80-year-old Afro-American woman and her family. It is a metaphor of America—genealogical, historical, autobiographical, and societal— assembled in such a way that it can be seen as a social history of Afro-Americans from slavery into the twenty-first century. The historical data was gathered from books listed in the bibliography. Other materials came from a variety of sources: documents from the Archives of Georgia and Alabama; correspondence and census tracts; birth, death, and marriage certificates; newspapers, and conversations with my grandmother.

One of the most valuable resources used was an audiotape of the family history that was recorded by my cousin, Homer Smith. He was listed as having been six months old in the 1900 census of the place in Georgia where my family lived. He died when he was in his late eighties. I am also indebted to family members in Detroit for additions to this information. Special thanks go to my cousin, Lois Gainous, R.N., M.S., for having compiled that historical data in the form of a booklet. I am also glad to have a childhood playmate and relative, Aunt Corine Wright, still alive to verify childhood memories. Additionally, the letter that my mother wrote to my youngest son about the family's flight from Georgia stands as a written document of truth. I am also deeply grateful to Evelyn S. Wallace, an Afro-American in Alabama, for permission to use her poem, "Be Proud," in this book. It describes beautifully how Afro-Americans should feel about themselves and their heritage.

This is not a book of fiction. The names and quotes of family members are authentic. There was good reason to omit the surnames of family members and the true name of the place in Georgia where my family lived: This was done to protect the privacy of family members, especially those who still live in Georgia. Literary and artistic license were taken in depicting events surrounding slavery. These descriptive events, traditions, and places were based on interviews with former slaves, as given in "Slave Interviews," edited by John Blassingame. I also used traditions of slavery, as told to me by my grandmother. Failing both, I used probabilities. Although I did not know all of the hereditary and environmental influences on my ancestors, I could only make assumptions based on the extrapolation of facts that were obtained from historical documents. Furthermore, different terms were used in this book for Black Americans as they were used at particular times in history and as this family history evolved. The term "Negro" is used in the time and place in history that is appropriate; likewise, the terms "Colored" and "Afro-American."

My purpose in writing this book was to share with others what life has taught me. I hope that my telling of the accomplishments of my family, while being handicapped by racism, will inspire others to strive to reach their greatest potential. Also, I hope that the book will leave an appreciation of Afro-Americans' evolution as a people.

TABLE OF CONTENTS

THE GOOD, THE BAD, AND THE UGLY

IN THE BEGINNING

My Grandmother, Mamie Veal Burney, at the age of 75

CHAPTER I
The Search Begins

Grandmama and I had as close a relationship as any first-born grandchild can have with a grandmother. In spite of this, she never talked about her life as a girl or as a young woman, until one day in 1951. I was in my early twenties when she told me that she hadn't known that she wasn't White until she was 12 years old, living in Georgia in the late 19th century. I asked, "Grandmama, how did you find out that you were Black?" She said, "I had chosen a little White boy that I wanted to marry, but I was told that I could not marry him because I was Black."

I never forgot that conversation or the picture it rendered. The idea to research my family's background began on that day. However, I did not actually start my research until a few years ago when I discovered that my great-grandfather was named Peter Veal. He was born around 1845, the son of a slave and a White man on the plantation of Mr. Veal in Wilkerson County, Georgia.

The Veal plantation was one of the most beautiful estates in this part of Georgia. Majestic oak trees lined the path to the house. Their branches reaching across the path to the house provided a magnificent arch. The house was of Southern Colonial architecture. Large white columns across the front of the house reached beyond the second-floor veranda to the roof. The well-kept lawn was dotted with graceful weeping willows and with ancient live oak trees whose branches dripped with Spanish moss. Behind this beautiful estate, as far as the eye could see, were many slave cabins and fields of cotton on these 3,500 acres. This is where the ugliness of slavery was seen.

Peter Veal became a house servant. He escaped the beatings and back-breaking work of the cotton fields because of his light skin color. Simply speaking, he was a "house nigger." This practice of differentiation by skin color was the beginning of a self-hate by many dark-skinned Negroes who thought that they must be inferior because of their color. After all, the light-skinned slaves did not have to work from sun-up to sun-down, picking cotton or doing other back-breaking work. A former slave in "Slave Interviews," edited by John W. Blassingame, stated that, "Yellow slaves thought that they were better than the Black slaves. The darker slaves, real Blacks, were ashamed of themselves when they were with Whites or Brights." This differentiation and shame occurred because the masters thought that slaves of light complexion were more clever servants and therefore more valuable. This idea of yellow skin being better than Black skin was intentionally instilled by the masters to put a wedge in slave relationships in order to keep the slaves under control. According to Grandmama, she often heard her father say that he hated "that one drop of nigger blood" in him. Less obvious circumstances of slavery, such as working in the master's house rather than in the fields, had given him this sense of superiority.

Peter was fortunate in having a good master. Although he was treated well overall, there is no substitute for freedom. One of the easier tasks that he performed was driving Mr. Veal to other plantations in the horse and buggy. He drove him in all seasons, but nothing compares to spring, the most romantic season in the Deep South. Nothing can compare to a balmy spring night when the air is heavy with the fragrances of magnolia, peach, and plum blossoms. This is a time made for love.

On a day like this Mr. Veal instructed Peter to hitch up the horse and buggy for a trip to the Graggs' plantation 10 miles away. Upon arriving, Peter "tied up" the horses and went to the back door of the house, into the kitchen. The servants made him very welcome. As he looked around the room, his eyes fell upon the most beautiful girl he had ever seen. He was smitten. He stood there with his mouth open, staring at her. She was a mulatto whose background was the same as his. Her father was White, and her mother was a slave. Everyone laughed at the look of awe on his face. They told him that her name was Sally. Sally and Peter talked the entire time that Mr. Veal and Mr. Graggs conducted their business. As he left, Peter told Sally that he would come to see her again.

Peter searched his mind for a way to visit the Graggs plantation again. He learned from other slaves that the Graggs' slaves held a semi-private church service for themselves. It was semi-private based upon a pretense of ignorance: both the master and the slaves pretended that the master did not know about the services. Because slaves had to have passes in order to visit slaves on other plantations, Peter decided that this would give him a chance and an excuse to visit Sally.

He usually attended the White Methodist Church with other slaves from the Veal Plantation. Mr. Veal was a steward in the Methodist church. The slaves did not need a pass to attend the White churches but had to sit in a special place in the loft. A different sermon was preached to them than to the Whites. The slaves were told to obey their masters and behave themselves so that they would go to heaven when they died.

There were several slave ministers who could read. The fact that any slave could read was a well-guarded secret because the masters did not want any slave to know how to read. However, those slaves had been introduced to Christianity in Africa by the missionaries. Jomo Kenyatta, first president of Kenya, said, "When the missionaries came, the Africans had the land and the Christians had the Bible. They taught us to pray with our eyes closed. When we opened them, they had the land and we had the Bible." It was this faith that sustained the slaves through the brutality of slavery.

Peter walked the 20-mile round trip to the Graggs' plantation to attend slave church services with Sally every weekend. After the services, which lasted several hours, they would socialize outside under the trees, when weather permitted. Sometimes, they enjoyed food that had been prepared in the cabins. Peter and Sally fell deeply in love while spending this time together.

One Sunday, when they were still in their teens, Peter asked Sally to marry him. They married in spite of the circumstances governing slave marriages. Slave marriages were not recognized by slave owners, and slaves could not live together as a couple if they were from different plantations. One of the peculiarities of the slave system was that members of a slave family often belonged to different masters. Fortunately, husbands at least were permitted to go to the wives' cabins on Saturdays. This meant that Peter had to have a pass to walk the 20-mile round trip to see his wife.

The Civil War had already begun when Sally and Peter married. Their first child, a boy whom they named George, was born during the last year of the war. Sally was spared the usual treatment of pregnant slaves because she was a "house nigger." Most slave women had to work in the fields from daylight until sundown throughout their pregnancies. Sometimes, the mistresses would ask the masters to reduce the work hours for pregnant females, who often delivered their babies in the field. All female slaves were given three months' free time from field work to nurse their babies.

During Sally's pregnancy, Mr. Veal served in the Confederate army, where he lost his life. The South, including Georgia and the Veal plantation, were devastated by the war. This plantation was no longer the beautiful well-kept estate it had been before the war. Mr. Veal's oldest son, Billy, was fortunately to return from the war. Billy, his mother, and the slaves worked hard to keep things going on the plantation. Although Peter and Billy played together as children and called each other by their first names, this relationship changed when Billy returned from the army. Due to the custom on Southern plantations, he began calling Peter "Boy." As part of this custom, old slaves were called "Auntie" or "Uncle." Any Whites who did not follow this custom would be severely rebuked by their families or their communities. Billy's calling Peter "Boy" hurt Peter deeply and caused him to feel very bitter.

On January 1, 1863, Abraham Lincoln declared that

four million slaves were free. However, many slaves did not know that they were free until two years after emancipation. Although slaves were kept in the lowest ignorance possible, many were more intelligent than they appeared to the Whites. Former slaves came from other communities to tell those still in slavery what they knew about the emancipation.

Some White landowners—the former planters—did not want the slaves to know that they were free. They needed this free labor because of a desperate shortage of money in the post-war South. Many masters went so far as to say that the slaves did not want to be free. Some slaves also said they did not want to be free, because they had nowhere to go and did not know what to do. However, they were lying. Lying was the prevalent action during slavery. It was Paul Lawrence Dunbar who said, "We wear the mask that grins and lies." Both slave master and the slaves had their hidden agendas —the master for hiding information and the slaves for lying because they needed each other. By 1865, the laws of the land demanded that all slaves be set free.

Many slave owners went to church with their slaves to help them celebrate their freedom. Many of these planters allowed their slaves to stay and work on their plantations and paid the slaves in crop shares as wages. Thus, sharecropping was established as a form of mutual accommodation.

Peter became a sharecropper for the Veal plantation. He told Sally, "At last we can live together with our son, George." Because this plantation was so large, he was able to build a cabin for his family in a very isolated area. He came to see "sharecropping" as the next best thing. He had privacy in his home life and more control over his work schedule.

Sally gave birth to five more children. They were born in quick succession after the birth of the first son. Through nature's natural birth cycle, there was about a two-year difference in their ages. There were two boys who were named Clifton and James, and three girls who were named Carrie, Ella Mae, and Mamie. Mamie, the youngest, would become my grandmother. Peter and Sally discussed the future for their family and established a mutual agreement that they all would work together. Sally, Peter, and all of the children, as they became older, worked in the fields. Everyone had to work because sharecropping left very little money for the cropper. Peter and Sally had many happy years together before she died shortly after the birth of Mamie.

Some time later, Peter married Natedell Shults, who was the daughter of a mulatto woman and a Jewish man. Natedell gave birth to five girls and two boys. The girls were Lulu, Lucia, Ada, Pearl, and Bessie. The boys were Andrew and William. The family continued to work together on the farm. Peter was eventually able to give 85 acres of land to each of his children. This family of light complexion continued to live a life of isolation.

It was not surprising, then, that Grandmama thought she was White. Upon entering her teens, she would meet John Solomon Burney, who would become my grandfather. This meeting would give a different meaning to her attitude about skin color.

CHAPTER 2
Grandmama and Grandpapa Meet

On a sunny fall morning, Peter took Mamie and her brothers to the general store to buy staples, dry goods, and feed for the livestock. At this time, after most of the crops had been harvested, the sharecroppers had a little money to buy their supplies and other necessities.

Mamie saw a striking-looking young Black man in the store. He was as black as a piece of coal, with silky black hair, an aquiline nose, high cheek bones, and deep-set eyes. She had seen very few dark-skinned Negroes because her family lived in isolation.

She was so intrigued by his looks that she did not hesitate to start a conversation with him. She asked his name and where he lived. He said, "My name is John Solomon Burney. Everyone calls me Solomon except my sisters and brothers, who call me Sol." He also told her that he lived on the Burney farm, which was in the same town and county as the Veal plantation. If a planter had fewer than 30 slaves, his place was not considered a plantation. The Burney farm had only 28 slaves. Although it has been romanticized that large, elegant plantations were everywhere in the South, they actually were outnumbered by smaller farms.

Solomon was as attracted to the pretty teen-aged Mamie as she was to him. They wanted to see each other again. However, both decided that it would not be a good idea for him to visit her father's house. Several factors contributed to this decision: skin color, several years' difference in age, and a stepmother with whom she did not have a close relationship.

Mamie and Solomon found places to meet during the next three years before their marriage. During these times together, he told her as much as he knew about his family. He told her that his father, Ned Burney, was a full-blooded Creek Indian slave; his mother was the daughter of a slave and a Creek Indian. He knew that Creek Indians had been taken as slaves during the war of 1812. This happened when their land was taken by troops led by Andrew Jackson from Tennessee and the followers of Colonel William McIntosh, Jr. from Georgia. The irony of this action was that McIntosh was the son of a Creek mother and a Scottish father.

Solomon had unpleasant memories of the more recent Civil War. He remembered Sherman's march through Georgia when he was a little boy, six or seven years old. Yankee troops inflicted great destruction on everything on the plantations. This devastation included the breaking of many barrels of sorghum syrup. Syrup ran down the ditches like water. Solomon and other little slave boys stuck their hands into the syrupy ditches and licked the syrup from their hands. That was quite a treat that tasted to them like food for the gods.

Solomon told Mamie more about his life and his family each time they met. He had left home around 1880 at the age of 17 after being given 80 acres of land. His father was able to give land to his children because he had worked on his master's farm for small wages after the war ended. His father worked hard all day and went to school at night, walking five miles each way. In only five months he learned as much as he could. Most important, he learned to read and write.

Solomon's parents, Ned and Jessie Mae, had five boys and one girl. The boys were named Henry, Crawford, Solomon, Matthew and Jordan. The girl's name was Matilda. Jessie Mae, their mother, died in childbirth when Jordan was born. Jordan himself lived only two months. After Jessie Mae died, other slave women took turns helping Ned with the youngest children. One woman was a wet-nurse for Jordan.

The woman Solomon came to think of as his mother was named Mimya. She had come to America with her mother, Sudee, on a slave ship when she was about ten years old. They came from people of Western Niger and spoke a Hausa language. Neither Mimya nor Sudee could speak English well. Their accents were so thick that Sudee was called Susie and Mimya was called Mary by the planter. However, Mimya never forgot her true African name.

Mimya and her mother were bought at a slave auction in Richmond, Va by Mr. Burney, a planter from Georgia. After the death of his wife, Ned was attracted to Mimya, this young, feisty, proud slave woman. He asked her to marry. When they married, his oldest daughter, Matilda, was about the same age as Mimya, in her early twenties. Ned's sons, Crawford, Matthew and Solomon, also came into this marriage. Henry, the oldest son, had been sold to another plantation owner. Together, Ned and Mimya had six additional children. The sons were Eddie, James and Newson; the daughters were Mattie, Laura and Minca.

Life was good for them for a short time. History tells us that life could be good only to a point for slaves. It was good in their love for each other and their children; otherwise, it was a cruel existence. However, what history does not tell us is that not all slaves were passive. Whereas some slaves enacted violent protests at times, many practiced passive resistance, which included shirking, faking illness, and abusing tools and other property. They were great at pretending stupidity or incompetence. All of these problems existed on most plantations and farms during this period.

CHAPTER 3
And They Stood in the Sun

The Ku Klux Klan (KKK) was founded in Tennessee in 1866 and became very active, with over 200,000 members. Focusing on the superiority of Whites, its goal was to keep former slaves from voting and exercising rights they had gained during Reconstruction. The Klan was composed of businessmen, professionals, and other Whites who wore hoods to hide their identities. In 1871 the Force Bill was passed, which used federal troops against the Klan. The KKK almost disappeared until 1915, when a clergyman established it as a protestant society. This new group expanded its hate to include immigrants, Jews, and Catholics. The Klan's type of membership and hateful practices have not changed in all these years and still exist throughout this country as small groups in some states. I hope that, one day, its members will understand that such hate is rooted in fear and that their fear, like any other, can be overcome so that they, too, can live in total freedom of heart and mind.

Former slaves enjoyed a small measure of freedom for a few years after the Civil War ended. This period was called the "Reconstruction Era." Freed slaves established political, educational, and religious organizations. They became teachers, lawyers, and doctors. Surprisingly to many, Negroes were in the Senate and the Congress in 1868 under Reconstruction laws. These legislators enacted laws that granted some protection to laboring people, especially farm workers. The laws helped Ned to acquire additional land. The KKK, of course, did not approve of any of these activities.

During this era of accomplishment, Mimya felt a great surge of freedom and insisted on being called by her African name. She had always hated the slave names that the planters had given to her. She told everyone adamantly, "MY NAME IS MIMYA."

In 1890, conditions in the Deep South began to deteriorate. It was the beginning of the end of the Reconstruction Era. W.E.B. Du Bois, author, activist and college professor, wrote, "The slaves went free, stood a brief moment in the sun—then moved back to slavery."

Florida passed the first "Jim Crow" law in 1897. (The term "Jim Crow" had its origins in minstrel songs. "Jim Crow" refers to the state legislature that wrote segregation laws.) In 1896, the doctrine of "separate but equal" had been validated by the United States Supreme Court in the case of Plessy vs. Ferguson. As a result, Jim Crow spread throughout the South like a plague; it was legal apartheid in the U.S.A. With it, Negroes were given a new name or label: we were now "Colored." There was true separation but no equality. We had separate waiting rooms at doctors' offices. In Atlanta there were separate elevators; in Mississippi, separate cemeteries. We were separated unequally in public accommodations, in everything the Whites could devise.

Circumstances also deteriorated for Ned and Mimya's family. Two sons and two daughters were still living at home when Ned dropped dead in his field in1898. The older son, Eddie, now 29 years old, assumed responsibility as head of the household. Cornelius, Mimya's sister, was also living in the home. The family had always worked hard, and this tragedy made them a closer family. By working together, they were able to keep their farm and other belongings.

Solomon had also acquired additional land during this short period of prosperity for Negroes. He built a wooden shack for himself near his father's home and was ready to settle down. On Christmas Eve in 1896, he asked Mamie to marry him. The day after Christmas, they applied for a marriage license and were married on Jan 1, 1897. He was 27 years old and she was 16. The next year, their first child, a daughter named Roberta, was born. They were very happy when a second daughter, Ara, was born a little over a year later.

However, tragedy was about to enter their lives again. One day, Roberta was quiet and listless. Mamie felt her forehead, which was hot to her touch. She tried to bring the fever down with home remedies, but to no avail. Roberta had diphtheria, and so did Ara. There was no cure for this disease. Both children died. The next child, a boy, was stillborn. Mamie never forgot this child. She talked about him to her oldest granddaughter, me, 50 years later.

Solomon and Mamie's family continued to grow. All of the children born while the family was in Georgia were girls: Pearl, Leona, Addell, Gertrude, and Willie Mae. As the family grew, Solomon bought more land. With his own hands, he built a nice home and put red wall-to-wall carpet on the living room floor. He also bought a blonde bedroom suite for Mamie. Their home had many books, one of which was the Bible.

At the end of the Reconstruction Era, Solomon had 2,000 acres of some of the most fertile land in Georgia. He was becoming a very prosperous farmer. Unfortunately, the Whites resented his ownership of this land; they wanted it for themselves and offered to buy it for nearly nothing. Solomon refused to sell. So, the Whites decided to take the land. They terrorized the family in every imaginable way. For example, they sicced a big dog on the oldest girl, who bit a huge chunk out of her leg. Finally, they threatened Solomon's life. He knew that he would be lynched if he didn't leave Georgia. He discussed this predicament with his stepmother, Mimya and his siblings. It was decided that his younger brother, Newson, would go ahead to Alabama and find a place where he and Solomon could live without the fear they had felt in Georgia. Newson went to central Alabama and changed his name to Roscoe Wright. When Solomon was told by Whites that he had to be out of town in 24 hours or die, he fled in the night. He planned to join his brother in Clanton, Alabama.

When Solomon left, Mamie and the girls moved in with Mimya. After a year in Alabama, Solomon had made enough money to send for his family. He met them at a train depot in a small place named Wardsworth, Alabama. They planned to stay there for a short time while he purchased furniture for the house he had rented in Mountain Creek.

Solomon was late in getting their luggage checked. The conductor of the train told him to "catch on to the last coach." In the process, Solomon's left foot slipped under the train and was mangled to the extent that it had to be amputated. The family lived in Wardsworth until Solomon's leg healed and he learned to wear his artificial leg. He was finally able to join his brother, Newson, AKA Roscoe Wright, in Clanton, Alabama. Solomon changed his name to Gus Wright, and Mamie changed hers to Mary Wright. The entire family lived under the surname of Wright and assumed names for the remainder of their lives. Not only did they lose their land and identities, Solomon also lost his family. He never saw Mimya and his other siblings again.

Solomon was down but not beaten. He bought a house in Clanton, learned the trade of shoe repair, and began all over again his active life of accumulating land. Mamie found a job as head cook in the town's hotel. The girls grew up and finished high school in Clanton. Willie Mae and Leona found suitors and married while living there.

Two additional children were born to Solomon and Mamie in Clanton, a boy named Johnny Levi and a girl named Corine. This only boy was the "apple of everyone's eye" and was always called "Brother." Brother and Corine did not know their real surnames until long after their parents had died. The older children let their parents take this family secret to their graves. Bits and pieces of the family's secret began to filter out after Grandmama's death in 1962. The most concrete information was found in a letter that my mother wrote to my youngest son in February 1975, the year before she died.

Before Mamie had left Georgia to join Solomon in Alabama, she sold the 85 acres of land that her father had given to her. She added this money to what she and Solomon were able to save. They used it to send the three older girls—Pearl, Gertrude and Addell—to Selma

University in Selma, Alabama. Selma University, one of the oldest Black junior colleges, was founded in 1878 by the Alabama Baptist Convention to train ministers and teachers.

It was when Pearl—my mother and the oldest daughter—graduated from Selma University that the family began to branch out. Pearl went from Clanton to Anniston, Alabama. In the next few years, other sisters followed. Finally, Grandmama and Grandpapa (Mamie and Solomon Burney) moved with the two youngest children to Anniston.

NEW LIVES

CHAPTER 4
Our New Hometown

The first school in which Mother taught was the Calhoun County Training School. It was in a small Colored community called Hobson City, located between Anniston and Oxford, Alabama, on the city bus line. The placement service at Selma University was instrumental in getting this position for her. The faculty looked forward to Mother's arrival. She had been very highly recommended as a Magna Cum Laude graduate. The University had also secured lodging for her with Mr. and Mrs. Turner.

When Mother arrived in Hobson City, there wasn't much to see. She had left Clanton, a very small place that had a population of about 6,000. This new place, Hobson City, wasn't nearly as large. She learned soon that the citizens of Hobson City were proud of their community, no matter its size. They called it an all-Colored town. Its biggest "claim to fame" was a beautiful park that had picnic shelters, a dance pavilion, a swimming pool, and large expanses of grass. Hobson City had two churches, a Baptist and a Methodist, and a grocery store. The citizens probably called it a city because it had an all-Colored police force, a circumstance that predated the writing of any Civil

Rights laws. Hobson City had homes that were nice and homes that were not.

Mother taught Latin, English, and sixth-grade Home Economics from 1923 to 1925 at the Calhoun County Training School. She attended the Baptist church with her landlady and became an active member who taught Sunday school and sang in the choir. She quickly caught the attention of the pastor, Rev. John Thomas Martin. Mother was pretty and 30 years younger. She was attracted to him because he was a dynamic, charismatic speaker who had a great sense of humor. Their age difference did not matter to them. He asked my mother to marry him after a short courtship.

Daddy was a widower whose wife had died after a lengthy illness. They were the parents of four sons: John Henry, Edward, Samuel, and Herbert. Edward died the year that my parents married, and Herbert died three years later. Samuel (S.J.B.) was 17, and John Henry, the oldest, was about the same age as Mother. These two sons went away to school or were in school when my parents married.

Mother and Daddy moved to Anniston during the first year of their marriage. I was born during this first year on a Sunday, which fell on Christmas Eve. That morning, Daddy preached the sermon and Mother sang in the choir. She started having labor pains right after morning services. Because this was her first child, she had mistaken these pains for a stomachache. Despite her growing discomfort and pain, she attended a 3 p.m. service, Baptist Young People's Union (BYPU), at 6 p.m., and an evening service at 7:30.

Mother, Daddy, Edgar, and I in 1927 –
I am four years old and Edgar is 2 years old

She knew now that she was having contractions, but she still thought she could make it back home to Anniston. I was born in Hobson City. Not until I was an adult and sent for my birth certificate did I realize that only Colored people considered Hobson City a town. My birth certificate listed my birthplace as Oxford, Alabama. My brother, Edgar, was born two years later in Anniston. He and I loved each other very much and were best friends, always.

In 1926, Mother began teaching at the 17th Street Public School in Anniston. This was the only school in town for all of the Colored children in both elementary and high schools. This was not good for a town with a population of 30,000. She taught Algebra, Latin, and English Literature there for 18 years and now had a two-year junior college, or associate, degree. She continued to attend college over the years during the summers.

Anniston is an industrial town with several pipe shops. During my childhood, there were textile mills, also. It touted itself as the "Soil Pipe Center of the World." Coloreds also lived in smaller outlying communities called Cobb Town, Sweet Valley, Thankful, White Row, and Union Hill. The majority of Coloreds lived in West or South Anniston. A small number lived between these two areas in a community called Zion Hill.

The Monsanto Chemical Co. was also located on the outskirts of town. When we were children, the stench of rotten eggs sometimes filled the air. We would brush it off with, "Oh, that's just Monsanto." We did not know anything about environmental hazards 70 years ago. However, awareness has grown in this area over the years. In 1996, the Alabama Department of Public Health declared Sweet Valley and Cobb Town public health hazards. Litigation has continued and finally paid off for the residents. The efforts of these citizens toward this litigation was reported in a widely published newspaper in this country and on national television.

Fort McClellan, an army encampment, also was located on the outskirts of town. A large White civilian population worked there. Coloreds did not work at Monsanto or Fort McClellan. Our men worked in the pipe shops at the hardest jobs and the lowest pay. We always knew that in any job we would be "the last hired and the first fired." Not only that, we also knew that we always had to prove ourselves first on a job.

In our communities all social classes lived together. A doctor lived next door to someone who worked at the pipe shop. A blue-collar wife worked as a domestic or perhaps did laundry for Whites. This situation gave children role models in their neighborhoods. It also meant that there were very nice homes owned by Colored professionals and businessmen in their midst; these people did not have to be quite as afraid of losing their jobs because they were allowed to serve only people of their own race. Most blue-collar workers intentionally did not paint their homes on the outside. As a result, many homes looked unkempt even though some of them were very nice inside, with nice furniture. An additional unwritten code was to "never let a White inside your house." To have let Whites know that some homes were nice would have jeopardized Coloreds' jobs. All things considered, we always felt that Whites did not want us to have anything. As Coloreds in the South, we grew up in a socially classless society. We had to care for each other because we didn't believe that anybody else would.

As in any other town or large city during the 30's, 40's and 50's, we had a Colored business strip. Anniston's was located on two to three blocks of 15th Street. Among the Colored businesses were a shoe repair shop, a dry cleaner, an insurance agency, a tailoring shop, a music studio, a beauty parlor, a photography studio, a restaurant, and a movie theater. White businesses also were found along this strip: a drug store, two grocery stores, and a restaurant with a White entrance on one side and a Colored entrance on the other. Most Coloreds did not patronize this restaurant.

We had a decent downtown area with several nice stores, many of them owned by Jews. The area also boasted a hotel, three movie theaters, and two supermarkets—a Jitney Jungle and an A&P. The tallest building in town had ten stories. We proudly referred to it as "the ten-story building."

Our religious faith was very strong, as indicated by the many churches in our neighborhoods. It seemed that there was church on every corner. In a four-block area of Mulberry Avenue were three churches: one Congregational and two Methodist. On Sunday morning at 10:45, bells would peal from each church. The most beautiful sounds came from Saint Michael's and All Angels Episcopal Church, where hymns were played with the chimes. Saint Michael's, a large church attended by Whites, was built in 1897. This stone building sits on half of a city block, surrounded by a low wall built of the same stone. It was in our community when I was a child and it is still there. Saint Michael's and All Angels Church is now the home of the Episcopalian Diocese of Alabama.

It was to this town of Anniston, Alabama, that my family came together to build a new life.

My childhood home in Anniston, Alabama

CHAPTER 5
Customs of the Old South

One day, Mother received a letter from her sister, Willie Mae. The contents of this letter brought her to tears. Aunt Willie Mae told Mother that her husband had walked out and left her and their toddler son, Leroy. Mother could tell that my aunt was devastated and humiliated because she was pregnant again. She wanted to know whether she could come and stay with us until she got on her feet. She was the first of the family to come to Anniston after Mother moved here. She left Leroy with Grandmama. The second child was stillborn.

Mother's sister, Addell, graduated from Selma University in 1925. She, too, found a teaching position, in Gadsden, Alabama, which was 30 miles from Mother in Anniston. Addell taught there for ten years, where she met her future husband. They had a family of nine children when we were growing up.

The last of Mother's sisters, Aunt Gertrude, graduated from Selma University in 1927. This was a significant year in our family's life. Grandmama and Grandpapa bought a house five blocks from our home. They moved to Anniston with little Leroy, who was not yet two years old; Brother, who was ten; and Corine, their youngest, who was three. Aunt Willie Mae and Gertrude moved in with them. Aunt Gertrude was able to get a teaching position in Anniston. She taught the fourth grade for many years. My grandparents had all of their children together again, except Aunt Leona, who had married in her teens while living in Clanton. She and her husband moved to Ohio in the early 1920s, where she gave birth to two daughters.

My brother Edgar and I grew up in this large extended family, of which Grandmama was the beloved matriarch. We always felt loved by everyone, even people in the community, because the "village" truly helped to raise us. Edgar and I were Preacher's Kids (PKs) and were expected to be perfect little children. I didn't resent this because the rest of the children were being raised by the same "village." This was part of the culture of our ancestors.

As children, we were born 60 to 65 years after slavery. Our grandparents were children of former slaves. To a great extent this affected our culture and upbringing. Children were very special because memories were still fresh in the minds of our grandparents and parents of the time when children were sold away from their parents. When a parent or parents were not able to provide for a child, there would almost always be someone in the community who would offer to raise the child. Another custom was to give children both a first name and a middle name. Many people were addressed by both names, such as "Carrie Belle" or "Willie Mae." Parents were proud to have the freedom to choose names for their children instead of having names assigned to them. When we migrated "up North," many of us dropped this part of our culture.

Another holdover from slavery was the practice of Whites addressing our men as "boy." To counteract this disrespect, many Colored men were addressed by their respective families as "Mister" in addition to their surnames. My aunts' husbands were always addressed by their wives, as well as by nieces and nephews, as "Mister." I never heard Mother call my father anything but Rev. Martin. My best friend, Inez, also said that she never heard her mother call her father anything but Mr. Lewis.

Another major influence on our upbringing was the Harlem Renaissance. This era existed through the 20's and the 30's. It was basically a psychology or state of mind in which we believed that our African heritage should be a source of pride and the foundation or social unity for all Colored people. Black writers and intellectuals were the leaders of debates about the conflicts of our true identity and how to achieve our destiny. Among these leaders were the poets Paul Lawrence Dunbar and James Weldon Johnson, the educator and writer W.E.B. Du Bois, the poet and writer Countee Cullen, and the writers Zora Neale Hurston and Langston Hughes.

Negroes and Coloreds, in whatever titles or labels we were given and whatever cities or towns we lived, were aware of activities that centered around Harlem. In the Deep South, the "Chicago Defender" and the "Pittsburgh Courier" (Colored newspapers) were shipped down to our towns and cities every week. These newspapers were read very eagerly. As a result, our parents knew about the Harlem Renaissance, and pride in our race was deeply instilled in us, in various ways. For example, it was common practice to hang calendars on the walls in our homes. However, in deference to our newly found racial pride, the only calendars that hung on our walls were of beautiful Colored people. This was our parents' way of teaching us that "Black is Beautiful." Also, I always had Colored dolls with which to play. Surprisingly, one Christmas, Santa brought a White doll to me. Evidently, Mother could not find a Colored doll that year. The next Christmas, Santa brought me the same kind of doll, but she had brown skin and black hair. I am certain that Mother gave Santa a hand in changing my doll's appearance.

Although we lived under racially repressive circumstances, our people stood tall with pride. Certain incidents that occurred during my childhood remain vivid in my memory. One day when I was a very little girl, I followed Grandmama out to a White farmer's truck parked across the street from her house. These farmers brought fresh produce into town to sell. As Grandmama approached the truck, the farmer asked, "What can I do for you, Aunty?" Grandmama summoned all the pride she could muster and answered the farmer in a voice dripping with icicles, "Oh, I didn't know that your mother and my mother were sisters." Without further verbal exchange, they conducted their business peacefully.

When I was a teenager, a third White grocer opened a store in our Colored business district. He was arrogant and disrespectful. One day, he did the unforgivable: he slapped the daughter of the tailor whose shop was next door to his own. She was home for summer vacation from Tuskegee University, which was also her father's alma mater. The news of what had happened traveled swiftly through our community. We were outraged and advised, "Do not shop at Mr. Brown's store again." This silent boycott closed down his business in a few weeks.

In the early 1950s, a similar incident occurred in the town's only hospital. All Colored patients, regardless of condition, age, or gender, were segregated to the Colored wing, where only Colored employees worked. The female employee assigned to Escort Services was instructed by a doctor to go to the Colored wing and bring that "nigger" who was scheduled for surgery. Angry, she quickly took the gurney to the Colored wing and brought it back empty. She told the doctor in her most innocent voice, "Doctor, I looked and looked, but I couldn't find a nigger anywhere." The doctor apologized and told her to go back and bring James Green, who was scheduled for surgery.

Despite some bad times, we had some good times, too. Our parents exposed us to as many educational and fun experiences as possible. Although we were denied access to the public library, the Congregational Church in our community filled the void by keeping a small selection of books in the basement of the church for us to check out.

When a small traveling circus came to town, Mother took us downtown to see the parade. Lions and tigers were in cages on flatbed trucks. We saw clowns, acrobats, elephants, prancing horses, and other animals as they marched down our main downtown street, with the animals leaving their "business" on the street along the way. This was as close as we came to a zoo when we were children. Mother also took my brother and me to the circus after it was set up for patrons. There, we saw a magic show and much more. Our special treat was a chance to ride Shetland ponies. Edgar was as excited as any little boy could be. I was terrified but didn't want Mother to know. I got close to the handler of the ponies and whispered, "Please put me on a slow pony."

A few days after our trip to the circus, Edgar started complaining about an earache. Mother tried several home remedies, but nothing eased the pain. She finally called the family doctor, who came to the house. He looked into Edgar's ear, used an instrument, and extracted a pea. The pea had swollen in the damp, warm recess of his ear. Mother and Daddy asked Edgar, "Why did you put a pea in your ear?" He answered, "I saw the magician at the circus put a pea in his ear and take it out of his nose." Needless to say, Edgar never tried that trick again.

Anniston was fortunate to have a small Museum of Natural History, which Coloreds were allowed to visit. Mother took us there often. The American Indian artifacts there were pointed out to us as being part of our ancestry. It was there that we were told that Grandpapa was part Indian. Afterward, we felt proud when we found Indian arrowheads buried in the back yard. We would excitedly show them to Mother.

I studied classical piano from age five to twelve. Daddy took me with him to the Baptist Sunday School conventions. I always took a piece of sheet music with me because, invariably, someone would ask me to play an instrumental (piano solo). I started playing the piano for churches when I was ten and continued until I finished high school. However, Edgar had the real musical talent. He played several instruments.

Despite growing up under adverse circumstances such as segregation and the Great Depression, we had a very happy childhood.

CHAPTER 6
The Enchanted Years

When Edgar and I visited Grandmama's house, as children, we felt that we were in the most wonderful place on this earth. We had our dearest playmates there. They were Corine, Mother's youngest sister, who was two months older than I, and Leroy, Aunt Willie Mae's son, who was the same age as Edgar. Grandmama's house was one of those unpainted homes with few amenities. It was always neat and clean. On Saturdays, she scrubbed the floors with lye soap and water. After she finished, the floors looked like pickled pine. She had a gramophone (record player) that she sometimes played for us.

She also had two beautiful beds that were from the better days of her life. They were mahogany with beautifully carved headboards that nearly reached the ceiling. The footboards were similar to those found on sleigh beds. Each bed had a thick feather "tick" (mattress). There is a similar bed in the Lincoln bedroom in the White House.

There was no grass in the front yard; therefore, it was swept every morning during warm weather. A large Sweet Shrub bush was on one side of the yard. This bush had maroon-colored buds that were a little larger than rosebuds. They had the most delightful scent. Little girls would tie buds in a corner of their handkerchiefs and put them in their dress pockets for perfume. On the other side of the yard was a large bush covered with small fuchsia-colored flowers that looked like miniature petunias. We called it a four o'clock bush because we believed that these flowers went to sleep at four o'clock in the afternoon. We waited until four o'clock, tapped each flower, and told it to go to sleep. The flowers would close their petals as though they really were asleep. In the morning, we would go out and find that the petals had unfolded and the flowers were awake. We sincerely believed that these flowers had gone to sleep on our command.

Grandmama did not work outside the home after she and Grandpapa moved to Anniston, so she was usually readily available to us. Grandpapa repaired the shoes of a few neighbors. He wasn't ever able to establish a good customer base because he worked from his home. His health began to fail soon after they moved there. Consequently, Aunt Gertrude and Aunt Willie Mae were the breadwinners.

One of my favorite memories of Grandmama is of her bustling about her kitchen while cooking. She could work magic on her wood-burning stove. It took a lot of skill to cook on one of those stoves. There were no dials marked "simmer" or anything else. She had to know which part of the top of the stove was the hottest and which had the least heat. She also had to know when the oven was at the proper temperature for baking. Her recipes were a handful of this and a handful of the other, a pinch of this and a pinch of that. She was a wonderful cook. She accompanied her kitchen activities by singing hymns in a low voice. Her favorite hymns were "Count Your Blessings," "When the Roll is Called up Yonder," and "Since Jesus Came into My Heart."

Clearly, Grandmama was a religious woman. In spite of everything that has transpired in the lives of our people, the church has always been the most important institution in our community. I was almost born in the church. I remember trying to understand the concept of Christianity as a child. When I was about six years old, I asked Mother, "If God is my father and God is Jesus' father, doesn't this mean that Jesus is my brother?" She answered, "Yes." What other answer could a parent give a young child?

Almost everyone started preparations for church on Saturday. This pre-preparation included making desserts and other dishes for Sunday dinner. We also chose the clothes that we would wear and made them presentable. We were lucky to have anything decent to wear during the Depression. Everyone tried to look as nice as possible out of respect for God's house, not to impress each other. Looking presentable for church is still a part of our culture.

Sunday services in our home began with breakfast. Edgar and I looked forward to this meal with both anticipation and dread. We anticipated the delicious food and dreaded the long prayer that Daddy would pray. This prayer delayed our getting to the food. In addition to Daddy's prayer, Edgar and I had to recite Bible verses. Being a precocious child, I always had a different verse every Sunday; Edgar always said the same verse, "Jesus Wept." We always had fried chicken. Mother could fry chicken that would make you want to eat the bones. We also had hot biscuits, fruit, eggs, and the mandatory grits.

Each Sunday, Edgar and I attended three services: Sunday school, 11 o'clock services, and B.Y.P.U., just as Mother and Daddy had done when Mother was pregnant with each of us. We also went to Vacation Bible School for a week and revival services five nights a week for two weeks during summer. I enjoyed all of this except revival services. All children who had not been "saved" had to sit on the "Mourner's Bench," which was the first pew in the church. When "the doors of the church were opened," I felt that the minister was directing to me personally his pleas to join the church, and I felt guilty. One night when I was seven years old, I went up and joined the 17th Street Baptist Church to ease my guilt. I had absolutely no other reason for joining the church.

The worst was yet to come. We were baptized on a Sunday afternoon at the 17th Street Baptist Church. All children were dressed in white robes and immersed in the pool beneath the pulpit. I did not really know what to expect and thought that I had met death when my head went under the water. I survived but have been afraid of water since that day. Although I did not know what I was doing when I joined the church at seven years of age, I have matured in my faith since then, every day of my life.

Our school was next in importance to the church in our community. Everyone believed that education was the hope for our future as a race. The year 1929 was very memorable in my life: the year that Corine and I started school and the year that the Great Depression began. Evidently, all children in the first grade, except I, had been taught to write their names before starting school. I was embarrassed to have to take my "Little Red Hen" reading book to the blackboard to copy my name, in which

Mother had written it. Needless to say, I learned to write my name in a very short time. We were taught to read by the phonics method. When I realized that sounds of letters form syllables and the syllables make words was the most magical day of my life. This meant that I could read anything that I wanted to read.

When I was nine years old, I was told that the book "Gone with the Wind" was in the Congregational Church library. I checked it out. It was the largest book that I had tried to read. I didn't think that I would be able to finish it because of its size. When I started reading this book, I couldn't put it down. I became an avid reader, and reading became one of the great joys of my life. After a few weeks, I was placed in the class for exceptional learners in the first grade.

There was a surprise waiting for Corine and me when we finished the first grade: Miss Brooks, our teacher, took us home to spend a week with her. She lived in Peidmont, Alabama, which is about fifteen miles from Anniston. She had a huge acreage of sugar cane. Corine and I sat mesmerized by the production of syrup in her back yard. The cane was fed into a large container. Then, horses walked around in a circle and somehow squeezed juice from the cane. The juice traveled a distance into a large, black iron pot that hung over a fire. The juice cooked down to syrup in the big pot.

Edgar and Leroy started public school two years later. After Edgar's first year, my parents realized that he had trouble learning. They obtained for him a tutor who was a member of the Congregational Church. Edgar attended the Lutheran school, which was a private elementary school. After he finished this school, he attended Calhoun

County Training School through the tenth grade and Cobb Avenue High in the eleventh grade. My parents and, most likely, the teachers had not heard of learning disabilities in those days.

Strict discipline and religion were taught in school, just as they were in our homes. I don't know whether the law of separation of church and state was in effect then. If it was, no one obeyed it. Every day, school began with the Pledge of Allegiance and devotions in each classroom. Devotions consisted of everyone repeating the Lord's Prayer, a scripture reading by the teacher, and everyone singing a hymn. I got into trouble about devotions at Christmas time in the fourth grade. Aunt Gertrude was my teacher. We had sung "Joy to the World" every morning for over a week. One morning, Aunt Gertrude asked me why I wasn't singing "Joy to the World" with the class. I said, "I am tired of singing that same song." She took me downstairs to Mother's classroom. Much to my surprise, Mother punished me. I was confused to be punished for doing what I had been taught to do, always tell the truth. I told the truth; I really was tired of singing that song.

As children, we grew up poor and often had to make our own fun. Summer was the best time of all seasons for doing a lot of fun things. Topping the list of our summer adventures was going to the woods. "Brother," our uncle, was our chaperone, baby sitter, and "naturalist." He was a teenager, seven years older, and we were still little children. Our little group consisted of Corine, Edgar, Leroy, and me. We would leave from Grandmama's house in the morning. As soon as we stepped off the sidewalk at Cooper Avenue and 19th Street, that was the end of the sidewalk. Everyone was barefoot except Brother and me. When I walked barefoot on the sidewalk, I felt as though I was walking on top of a hot stove. Walking on pebbles on the dirt road was also painful. We walked past a semi-factory town. There were about ten identical gray frame cottages on either side of the road. Whites who worked in the textile mill lived in these houses. When we walked a little farther, we entered the woods. There was soft, cool, gray sand under the trees. I was able to go barefoot for a short time on the sand. We walked under a great canopy of trees. The dappled sunlight streaming through these trees made delicate, lacy patterns on the ground. It was magical.

When we came from under the trees, I had to put my shoes on again. We brought buckets and baskets with us to gather edible wild berries and fruits from the woods. We always gathered wild blackberries and muscadines (southern grapes). Brother told us which berries and fruits were poisonous, so we avoided them. We also gathered sassafras roots from the sassafras trees. The roots were dried and used to make a hot tea, which we drank in the winter. Sassafras roots were also sold in the supermarket until they were found to cause cancer. Last, we gathered persimmons and hickory nuts in the fall.

As we walked, we had to cross railroad trestles. Brother always had to hold my hand because I was afraid that I would fall into what seemed to be an endlessly deep gully. One day, we saw huge black birds flying in a circle overhead. We asked Brother, "Why are those birds flying like that?" He told us that these were buzzards flying over something dead. Naturally, we had to investigate. We found that what Brother had told us was true. He also taught us to watch for snakes. It was not unusual for us to hike 12 or 14 miles a day.

When we got back to Grandmama's house, she always had pie plates lined with pastries on the kitchen table. She made pies from whatever fruit we brought from the woods. Also, we went to her house every Sunday during the summer for homemade ice-cream and cake.

One day, Brother told us that he would have a special treat for us after church on the next Sunday. He said that he was going to take us to see a band of Gypsies in the woods. He had been told that Gypsies would steal little children and anything made of gold. Of course, this wasn't true, but we didn't know. We came to a large clearing in the woods on that Sunday. The Gypsies, dressed in colorful clothes, were cooking a stew in a large black kettle similar to ones in which women boiled clothes on washday. I was very afraid of the Gypsies because I felt as though I had two strikes against me: being a little kid and wearing eyeglasses with gold earpieces. I clung to Brother's hand for dear life. Surprisingly, the Gypsies did not bother us. With a crowd watching them as though they were from another planet, the Gypsies probably thought that we were crazy. The women were pretty and the men were handsome.

We also looked forward to spring for the joy of flying kites. Brother and Grandmama would help us make our kites. Brother gathered small branches, which he tied together for the frames. He and Grandmama covered the frames with brown paper that had been saved from grocery bags. Grandmama made paste from flour and water to hold them together. She had saved bits of twine, tied them together, and rolled them into a ball for our string. She also put a tail in each kite, made from pieces of rags tied together. Obviously, the kites were not pretty but we loved them. Brother took us to the "old field" to fly our kites. The "old field" was a large open field surrounding the textile mill, about a block from Grandmama's house. What fun we had!!

CHAPTER 7
Hard Times

As the Depression deepened, even as children, we could see changes all around us. All that we didn't see or experience, we learned from overhearing our parents talk about the hard times everyone was experiencing. They talked about banks failing, insurance companies going bankrupt, businesses closing, homes being sold at tax sales, seeing furniture set out on the street, and continually rising unemployment. We decided that everyone was poor but that there were degrees of poverty. When you don't have food to eat, that is about as bad as it can get. We knew it was bad because there were soup lines in big cities all across the country.

The first change that I remember in our lives was that Daddy no longer was the pastor of one church full time. Instead, he was the pastor of two rural churches, one on the first and third Sundays and the other on the second and fourth Sundays. The members of his congregations were barely able to pay him a few dollars. They compensated as best they could. Those who didn't have money brought farm produce to the altar at church. On Sunday nights,

Daddy brought home fresh vegetables, fresh-churned butter, buttermilk, and sometimes a chicken. Mother didn't fare any better as a teacher. The Board of Education was unable to pay full salaries. Teachers were paid part salary and part warrants. Warrants were similar to promissory notes.

Needless to say, my parents needed a way to make more money. They found an answer right under their noses. We had a very nice, large home with many amenities. As the Depression deepened, my parents started renting out rooms. They rented the front bedroom to the principal of the Lutheran school. They rented their bedroom to Mrs. Foreman, my music teacher. They moved a daybed into the dining room for themselves. It was similar to a trundle bed, which became a double bed at night. Edgar slept on the davenport (sofa bed) in the living room, and I had a small bedroom. Although we had gas space heaters in every room, the only ones used were in the renters' rooms and the bathroom. A big pot-belly stove replaced the gas heater in the dining room. This room became our "great room." Edgar and I had no heat where we slept. The quilts that covered us were so heavy that we could barely turn over under them. They were made for warmth, not beauty.

Daddy had four large truck gardens that he cultivated alone in vacant lots in town as an aid in feeding our family. He had one garden on a corner lot that faced a billboard across the corner of the lot. Billboards were always at ground level in our small town. Food was stolen from this lot while the billboard hid the robbers' activity. Food was the most significant thing that our people stole in those days. Squirrels, pigeons, and pet rabbits or chickens also were fair game for the dinner table.

As an excellent seamstress, Mother started taking in sewing. I was her little assistant. I did all of the handwork and sewed on snap-fasteners; zippers hadn't been invented. I learned how to sew from watching Mother and made my first dress when I was ten years old. Most of the sewing was done on Friday night, all day Saturday, and often all of Saturday night. Some of her customers would come to our house on Sunday morning to get their garments to wear to church. On many Sunday mornings, Mother could not go to church because she hadn't slept. When she couldn't attend, she sent her tithes with me. This action made a lasting impression for me.

Mother had several White and Jewish customers in addition to her Colored customers. For example, she was dressmaker for the wife and daughter of a lieutenant colonel stationed at Fort McClellan. She made beautiful clothes for the daughter, who attended the University of Alabama. One of her Jewish customers had relatives who came down from New York City every summer. I think that they probably had ties to the garment district because they brought remnants of fabric with them. They gave Mother some of these remnants, which she sold. These Jewish relatives brought pictures of dresses they wanted made and the fabrics for them. Mother would take their measurements and fit the dresses before they left town. When she finished the garments, the relatives in Anniston paid her for her labor and shipped the dresses to New York.

One summer, Mother made a deal with the Singer Sewing Machine Co. They put six sewing machines in our home. Mother taught a sewing class and made an effort to sell the machines. She was able to earn a commission

49

from every machine that she sold. This activity took place in our dining room.

Life wasn't all fun and games for us when we were children. We worked hard. Edgar delivered prescription drugs on his bicycle for a downtown drug store. He and I kept the house clean as our chores. Daddy cooked Monday through Friday and most Saturdays. He taught me to cook during the summers that Mother attended summer school, and he took a vacation from cooking. I hated cooking when I was a child, and I still don't like it.

Mother would can or preserve about 100 jars of fruits and vegetables every summer. When she made jelly, it was my job to skim the scum off the jelly as it cooked. I didn't like this job, either. I have memories of a day when my parents, Edgar, and I sat in a circle in the back yard preparing to can a bushel of peaches. Daddy and Edgar were washing fruit jars. Mother and I were peeling and slicing peaches. After many hours of this work, I remarked, "My back is hurting." Daddy said, "Shut up, you don't have a back." I had no choice. I kept slicing and peeling peaches for what seemed to be forever. Grandmama also canned food. She made the most delicious watermelon rind preserves, and her peaches tasted like those canned by Del Monte. All of the food that we canned wasn't for our use. Some of it was intended to help feed others, including people who went from door to door begging for food. When Whites came to our door, I asked Mother, "Are we going to give food to them?" She said, "Yes, we help everyone."

My fondest memory of my father is the compassion he had for people in need. The majority of our people had small coal-burning fireplaces to warm their drafty homes. Those who were not able to buy coal would walk along the railroad tracks with empty burlap bags to pick up coal that had fallen off boxcars. Daddy would ask the owners of coal yards for bags of coal and owners of downtown stores for clothing, all to give to those in need.

These actions and attitudes by our parents taught Edgar and me great lessons in tolerance and compassion.

During the Great Depression, many of our people thought that any way out of their situation was better than staying in the South. They had been told that life was much better "up North." That claim was not really true, though. Northern Negroes were little better off than Southerners. Thus began the great migration to northern states. Most people from Anniston went to Chicago. I remember going to the train station with my parents to bid farewell to some of their friends. I heard one woman ask the ticket master for a one-way ticket to Chicago and add, "'cause I ain't never comin' back." There were about 20 people in this group. They had their belongings in cardboard suitcases and shopping bags. They had been told that they could live in the big northern cities for a year and be eligible for welfare. Welfare was denied to most Coloreds in the South. Many of these migrants did receive welfare and lived in the ghettos.

Ever since then, I've watched, listened, and formed a definite opinion about the welfare-payment system. Welfare reform has been instituted recently in this country. It has not been entirely successful, but it is a good thing and long overdue. Welfare has not done anything to keep the minority family intact. In my opinion, every citizen should have the dignity of making his or her own way with a living wage instead of a minimum wage. Although the welfare reform plan has fallen short in many ways, it should not be thrown out. Welfare reform needs to be reformed so that those who are able to work should work and be paid a living wage.

This was also the era when many light-complexion or mulatto Negroes went north and passed for White. I remember hearing family members speaking in hushed voices that Cousin Lily Mae's daughter had gone north to pass for White. Lily Mae was Grandmama's niece. Corine and I remember seeing Lily Mae when we were little girls. We both agreed that she looked exactly like a White woman. According to W.E.B. Du Bois, light complexions were the result of slaves who had been brought to this country and "co-mingled their blood with White and Red America that by this time, less than 25 percent of Negro Americans were of unmixed African descent."

We, too, went to Chicago in 1933, but for a different reason. The Anniston Board of Education finally had enough money to redeem some of the warrants that teachers had received instead of salary. We used this opportunity to go to Chicago for the World's Fair. Even better, this was a chance for Daddy to visit his two older sons, John Henry and SJB, who had lived in Chicago for several years.

This was our first experience in riding a train. Coloreds were segregated to the first coach behind the baggage car. Trains were fired by coal, and cinders flew into our coach. We couldn't eat in the dining car. A porter came through our coach with a basket of sandwiches, crackers, candy, etc. for sale. Many people brought lunches with them. As the train entered Chicago, the most awful odor came into the coach. I thought the odor was from someone's feet, but it turned out to be the odor from the animals in the stockyards.

We stayed with my half-brother, SJB, in Chicago. He was known as Father Samuel J. Martin, rector of Saint Edmunds Episcopal Church. At that time, the church was located at Michigan Avenue and 61st Street. He assumed full charge as the priest in 1929. We had a closer relationship with John Henry because he and Mother corresponded often. For Christmas, he gave me the prettiest dress that I had as a child.

We went to the World's Fair, but I don't remember anything that I saw. Afterward, Mother talked to her students for weeks about things she had seen at the Fair. What I do remember is visiting SJB's church. I didn't understand anything that was going on in the service, but I still remember the beautiful alter. There seemed to be 100 red votive holders containing lighted candles. It was an awesome sight to a little girl. I also thought that the vestments worn by my brother and the alter boys were beautiful. Added to this beauty were the lace mantillas that some of the women wore on their heads.

We enjoyed the trip but were happy to be back at home with our family.

CHAPTER 8
Growing Pains

Our little gang—Edgar, Corine, Leroy, and I—were growing up. We started looking about us and seeing life from our own perspectives, including views of other people. I never heard my parents say anything negative about other people, which included Whites, Jews, and people with non-heterosexual preferences. We were not taught hate and discrimination by word or deed in our homes, churches or schools. I will not say that we didn't develop a strong dislike and distrust for people who mistreated us. However, there is a big difference between dislike and hate. I decided as a child that Whites disliked Coloreds, Jews, Yankees, and foreigners, in that order, and that rednecks hated everybody. We, in turn, despised the Confederate flag and the song "Dixie" because they represented slavery to us.

As we entered our teens, our family ties remained strong. We looked forward to Aunt Addell coming from Gadsden to visit Grandmama. She always brought her children with her. My oldest cousin, Freddie, looked like Grandpapa, who we knew was three-quarters Indian. Because Freddie didn't look like us, we thought she was very pretty. We would say, "Look at Freddie. Ain't she pretty? She looks just like an Indian." As a part of our culture, girls were not told that they were pretty or attractive. Although Corine, my cousins and I were attractive girls, no one ever told us. All we heard was, "Pretty is as pretty does."

I always had to be a very responsible child. At the age of 13, I was given responsibilities that few children that age have to assume. One day, Mother told me that she and Daddy were going into the hospital at the same time for major surgery and that I would have to take care of Edgar. She had put money in a checking account for me. I was to withdraw this money as needed to buy food to cook for Edgar and me. At that time, I was too young to realize the seriousness of this situation—that Edgar and I could become orphans. The realization hit me when I visited Mother at the hospital. She was coming out of anesthesia, which was ether in those days. Colored patients were put in a frame, one-story building behind the Southern Colonial-style brick hospital reserved for Whites. Mother was not allowed in the recovery room of the main hospital. Seeing her there was a frightening sight; I truly thought that she was dying. I started screaming and crying so loudly that workers had to take me out of the hospital.

Both of our parents were in the hospital for about two weeks. It was unheard of in those days for a patient to be allotted a certain number of hours of hospitalization for major surgery. Mother recovered quite well, but Daddy did not. She called Edgar and me together and told us that Daddy was terminally ill with cancer. She also said that the doctor had given him only three months to live. To our joy, however, he lived three years and never went back into the hospital. I realize now that those three years must have been terrible for him. He was left alone most of the day because Mother had to go to work and we had to go to school. Toward the end when the pain got so bad, a woman was trained and hired to check on him and administer shots of morphine.

After Daddy became ill, life changed dramatically for us. We didn't have roomers anymore. The principal of the Lutheran school married, and the music teacher bought a building in which she lived. We still had enough food, but not the abundance and variety that we had enjoyed. Still, I don't remember ever being hungry. What I do remember is getting tired of having peanut butter and cracker sandwiches and a baked sweet potato every day for our brown-bag school lunches. One day, Edgar and I were told that we would be allowed to eat the free hot soup lunch that some students were getting. That soup was delicious!!

Mother stopped sewing dresses and started making furniture slipcovers. I asked her why she had changed plans. She said, "I just got tired of making dresses." I know now that she made the change because she could earn more money in a shorter time. I was her assistant in this endeavor, just as I had been when she had made dresses. I sewed on snap-fasteners and pressed the pleats around the bottoms of the slipcovers. Sometimes, Edgar and I would go to the customers' homes, where I would put the slipcovers on the furniture and collect the money. Although times were really hard for us, we were able to keep our home, and Mother always had food on the table.

The Anniston Board of Education realized that we had outgrown our existing public school. A new high school was built for us on Cobb Avenue and aptly named Cobb

Avenue High School. Built of brick, with nine rooms, it was much better than the former facility but totally unequal to the White high school. Our teachers coped with the inequities in our schools, just as our parents coped with the inequities in our lives. They were the most dedicated teachers, our greatest gift in the school, who had total cooperation from our parents.

We did not have a gymnasium in the new school, but that did not keep us from having physical education classes. We did calisthenics outdoors when the weather permitted and also had basketball tournaments. We did have a place for assembly, though. Folding doors between two classrooms were opened for this activity, which kept us from having to go outdoors again.

The Home Economics room contained an old gas stove, one treadle sewing machine, and a long table. We took turns learning how to use the sewing machine and made a variety of seams. We also learned about nutrition but had only one demonstration cooking class—to make a soufflé, of all things, something that we probably would never make again—using ingredients that the teacher must have brought from home. At least, that opportunity introduced us to the use of a recipe. In addition, we were taught self-esteem in our schools. I especially remember a class in my senior year. Our teacher told each student to say what he or she thought was an outstanding trait in another student in the class. This taught us that each of us was wonderful in some way.

All students took college preparatory classes because we had no other choice. Latin was our foreign language. We studied chemistry, although we had no chemistry laboratory. When I arrived in college, I was frustrated that my high school chemistry teacher had not taught me to solve problems. However, it wasn't long before I realized that a laboratory was necessary to solve chemistry problems, and my high school couldn't have taught problem solving without a laboratory.

My favorite teacher in high school was Miss Louise Moses. She taught English Grammar and English Literature. I enjoyed diagramming sentences almost as much as kids today enjoy playing video games. I still remember many of the quotations we had to memorize that were written by great authors. She made everything that we studied very interesting. She put love and romance into anything that she could. As teenagers, we loved that. When we studied Shakespeare's works, we learned about his life. As a class project, we made a replica of the Globe Theater where his plays had been performed.

Music appreciation, which was taught by Mrs. Lillian Foreman, was a favorite subject of most students. Mrs. Foreman was the widow of a doctor and had studied at the Chicago Conservatory of Music. In her classes, she taught the four choirs of the symphony orchestra and every instrument in each choir. She played solo recordings of each instrument, and we had to identify the instrument and the choir to which it belonged. I sang in the school choir, which she directed. Most of the songs that we sang were Negro spirituals. We also sang a few folk songs and the "Hallelujah Chorus" from Handel's "Messiah."

The school choir sang at the high school Baccalaureate and graduation services. We also sang Negro spirituals at the emancipation services held every January first at the 17th Street Baptist Church. The first two pews in the center section of the church were reserved for Whites who came to these services. As a child, I thought that they came just to hear us sing spirituals so that they could be reminded of slavery. I realize now that this was not the case. They came as a tradition of the old South, when some masters went to the Negro churches to help the slaves celebrate their freedom. Our visitors were still participating in this celebration 65 years after the signing of the Emancipation Proclamation by President Lincoln.

I will always appreciate Mother for letting Edgar and me grow up to be normal teenagers instead of PKs (Preacher's Kids). It seemed that everything that was fun was a sin to Daddy. Among these things were movies, dancing, blues, and jazz. In spite of this, Edgar went to the Noble Theater every Saturday to see the serial Westerns. I didn't like Westerns; therefore, I would go to the Ritz or Calhoun Theater on Sunday afternoon to see a good movie, after telling Mother that I was going to Sunday afternoon church services. She probably knew that I wasn't telling the truth. It was easier for Edgar to have a believable reason for his activities on Saturday.

Dancing was always one of the joys of my life. One night, after a basketball tournament, a boy named Paul asked me to dance. I told him that I didn't know how to dance. He said, "Just move the way I do," and I did. This was the only introduction that I had in learning how to dance, and I never stopped enjoying dancing. Many kids went to the Juke Joint to dance after school. Only teenagers went to this one-room place that had a jukebox. It was run by a woman and her teenage son, named Ben. Cold drinks, candy, cookies, etc. were also sold there. I would go there every week day after I did my chores and homework. My curfew was 10:00 p.m. The women who lived nearby the

Juke Joint called Mother to report that I was there dancing. After the third time that Mother received one of these calls she told me about them. She did not chastise me; instead, she was angry with the women who called. She had told them, "I would rather that she be there dancing than doing other things that are much worse."

I always liked the blues that I heard from the big green frame house across the street. I wasn't allowed to sing the blues or play them on the piano. However, my girlfriend and I would slip out to the White Row, an outlying area, to hear the men sing the blues and play their guitars.

Being out among other teenagers usually guaranteed us a good time. Of course, Edgar and I had both friends and more-than-friends of the opposite sex. I always thought that my brother was very handsome. The girls evidently agreed because he certainly had no shortage of girlfriends. Similarly, the boys and I had mutual admiration for each other, sometimes as just friends, sometimes as more. Officially, I wasn't allowed to "receive company" until I was a senior in high school. However, I had boyfriends before then, unknown to my parents. Edgar was instructed to chaperone me on my dates, but neither Edgar nor I liked that arrangement. My date, Edgar and I always left home together but parted soon thereafter. Then, Edgar agreed to meet us at a designated place early enough for the three of us to get home before my curfew ended. Edgar and I always covered for each other.

There were sad days in high school, as well as fun days. For example, we were very sad to see very bright students have to drop out of school to go to work in order to help support their families. "Brother," our uncle, had to drop out of school in the ninth grade for this reason. Jobs became available through programs that President Roosevelt and Congress established. One program that I remember was the Works Progress Administration (WPA), which paid $3.00 a week. These small wages were better than nothing. Brother worked as a carpenter in the Civilian Conservation Corp. (CCC).

This was also a very sad time for our extended family. Grandpapa was confined to his bed with a heart condition for the last year of his life. Grandmama did not leave home that year, 1936. On Christmas Eve, she decided that she would make a quick trip downtown to do some shopping for the holiday. While she was gone, Grandpapa died in Aunt Willie Mae's arms. As children, we said to each other that Grandmama and Grandpapa loved each other so much that Grandpapa couldn't tolerate giving in to death until Grandmama was not at home to be a witness.

Life went on. I continued to be a good student. I was valedictorian when I graduated from junior high and salutatorian when I graduated from high school. An honor award was given to me as the most all-around student in high school. I was a member of the Junior Music Study Club, the Junior Federated Women's Club, and the Junior N.A.A.C.P. (National Association for the Advancement of Colored People) because Mother had urged me to do so.

On the day of my graduation from high school in 1940, Mother called me into Daddy's room so that he could see me in my cap and gown. She said to him, "You told me that you would not live to see this little girl graduate from high school. She is graduating today, and I bought her the gold watch that you said you would give to her if you were still alive." Daddy died two months later.

Proud to be Proud

After Daddy's death, Mother told me about a promise that she had made to Daddy when I was born. She had promised him that she would never let me work in the "White folk's" kitchen because Daddy's parents, William and Emmaline Martin, had been slaves in Chambers County, Alabama. As slaves and freed slaves who had remained on the plantation as farm hands seven years after slavery was abolished, they had first-hand knowledge of slave women who were raped by slave masters and their overseers. They shared this knowledge with their children in the hope that they and theirs would not suffer a similar fate. Daddy had five brothers—Frank, William, Gus, Lewis (Pick), and Robert—and one sister, Viola. The only members of Daddy's family that I knew were his brother, our Uncle Bob and his nephew, Lewis Jr., both of whom lived in Anniston. Armed with that promise, I would make a better life for myself than to work in someone's kitchen.

All that I am and all that I ever could be, I owe to the LIFE LESSONS taught to us by our parents. They instilled in us integrity, moral values, pride, and deep faith. These are some of the lessons we learned:

HONESTY: One day, Daddy sent Edgar and me to sell green beans door to door. When we had sold nearly all of the beans, most of those left were in bad condition. Edgar decided to put the bad beans on the bottom for the last customer. I tried to talk him out of doing this but he did it, anyway. The customer called our house and reported to Daddy what we had done. When we got home, Daddy started reprimanding us for this dishonesty. I insisted, "I didn't do it! Edgar did it!" Edgar was punished. On another occasion, Mother wasn't at home. I answered the telephone and heard a White man on the line. He asked me to tell his wife a lie and promised to pay me a dollar for doing so. When Mother came home, I told her about the call with great excitement because of the money involved. She was furious and told me that I wasn't going to do anything like that now or ever again. I had thought she would be happy about the money because a dollar was a lot of money in those days; but she said that money does not come before honesty.

MANNERS AND RESPECT: "Please," "Thank you," "Excuse me," and "May I" were natural parts of our vocabulary. We had no choice but to use these phrases at the proper times. Unfortunately, manners and respect seem to be a lost art today.

VENGEANCE: At some point I must have indicated a strong wish to repay those who had hurt me when I was a child. As a result, I can still hear my mother say in the voice of God or at least Moses, "'Vengeance is mine, I'll repay,' sayeth the Lord. If you try to repay people for their meanness, you will be taking God's work out of His hands and God won't like that." I have lived long enough to see that God's vengeance is greater than anything I could ever do to anyone. Therefore, I leave vengeance to God.

CHRISTIAN RESPONSIBILITY: Daddy often stressed to us that we must always give God His part of our time, talent, and money and always have a "church home."

GRATITUDE: If my brother and I started complaining about what we didn't have, Mother would say to us in a stern voice, "If you aren't grateful for what you have, that which you seem to have will be taken away from you." I believed my mother then, and I still believe that this admonition from her has kept me from being materialistic.

RACISM: We lived in a society that was so segregated, I did not realize that racism existed until I was ten years old. I learned about racism when Mother took Edgar and me downtown on the city bus for the first time. When we got on the bus, I sat in the first empty seat I saw. Mother told me that I couldn't sit there and took us to the back of the bus. I asked her, "Why can't I sit in that seat?" She said, "I'll explain this to you when we get off the bus." When we got off the bus, she pointed to a filthy White woman and her equally filthy little girl. Mother said, "As you know, you and Edgar had a bath and put on clean clothes before you left home. But that woman and child would not want you to sit next to them; they think that you are dirty and not good enough to sit there because of your race. Really, though, you are clean and as good as anyone else." I never forgot my mother's words and have never felt that I was inferior to anyone because of my race.

SUCCESS: Edgar and I were told by our parents before we reached our teens, "In order to be a success as a Negro in America, you have to be as good as best and better than the rest." Nothing has changed in the last 70 years. We knew from an early age that these words meant hard work and doing all tasks to the best of our abilities. Accordingly, we also were told that we could do whatever we wanted to do and be whatever we wanted to be in life. Edgar and I believed these words.

TRUTHFULNESS: One night, I didn't quite make it home before my curfew. Cousin Leroy came by our house, and Mother asked him whether he knew where I was. He didn't know, but he told a tall tale. Edgar came home next. He told a second version of where I was. When I came home, Mother was sitting on the front porch, waiting for me. When she asked me where I had been, I gave a third version of my whereabouts. Mother could hardly keep from laughing. Then, she quoted a great author who wrote, "Oh, the tangled web we weave, when first we practice to deceive." She also explained, "When you tell one lie, it leads to another lie; and soon, you don't know what the first lie was about, so always tell the truth."

THRIFTINESS: I think that the Depression made some of us too thrifty. No matter how much we accumulated, we always felt poor because we remembered poverty. My parents' favorite expression was, "Pennies make nickels, nickels make dimes, and dimes make dollars." I learned to save!

GOSSIP: If Mother overheard me gossiping with my girlfriends on the telephone, she would make me hang up. She would say, "A dog who brings a bone will take a bone." As a result, I have never been much of a gossip.

ACCOMPLISHMENTS: Daddy taught us that we should never talk about our accomplishments. This was a part of our southern culture. I agree with a popular talk-show hostess who was taught the same thing and believes that children need to be given the opportunity to be proud of their accomplishments.

GOOD DEEDS: We also were taught that if we did good deeds, we were not to go around talking about them. This admonition is backed by scripture.

Upon graduating from high school, I was about to go out into the world, away from the security and love of my family. I would experience some unbelievable, trying times, but these LIFE LESSONS would sustain me.

THE GOOD, THE BAD, AND THE UGLY

"BE PROUD"

By Evelyn S. Wallace

Be proud of who you are
Don't waste your time being jealous or rude.

Be kind when you speak of others
You'll get nowhere with a bad attitude.

Be proud of what you can do
Don't forfeit your chances to excel.

Take pride in the things around
Be confident and you will do well.

Be proud of your family roots
It's the one thing you cannot change.

You can choose your friends but not your family
Be respectful and proud to carry the name.

Be proud of your accomplishments
No matter how small the praise.

Do the best you can with what you have
You'll be rewarded in so many ways.

I, Mary Martin, am a freshman at Tuskegee Institute

CHAPTER 9
College Days

In the spring of my senior year in high school, Mother gave me a bulletin from the Tuskegee Institute (Tuskegee Universtiy). She instructed me to look through it and decide which course of study I wanted to have as a major. We did not have counselors at our school to help me with such a decision. The only professional Colored women I had seen were either teachers or nurses. I decided that because I could cook and sew, I would major in Home Economics. I had no choice in the decision of which college I would attend. As far as my mother was concerned, I would attend one of the best colleges that she knew about. I shall be eternally grateful to her because she didn't listen to me when I told her that I wanted to attend a different Colored college in Alabama with my friends.

One bright, sunny day in September 1940, Mother and I rode the Greyhound bus to the Tuskegee Institute in Alabama for my enrollment as a freshman. This was my first experience on a college campus. I was very impressed by what I saw. I was more impressed when I learned about the history and the founding of Tuskegee Institute by a former slave, Booker T. Washington, in 1881. The school opened on July 4th of that year with one teacher, 30 students, and a few shack-like buildings. After 25 years, there were 83 buildings on 22,000 acres. The amazing fact was that all of these buildings were built by students who had been taught to make the bricks and install electricity for the buildings. Students also made the dormitory furniture.

I was equally impressed by an especially beautiful building with huge, white, Greek columns. It also had sweeping stairs ascending from each side that led to a flat plane, from which central stairs led to the entrance. This building was Tompkins Hall, the central dining hall for all students.

There were large expanses of lawn on the campus, dotted with magnificent old trees. Farther out on the campus were the trade buildings. Among trades taught were printing, shoemaking, carpentry, tailoring, building construction, and auto mechanics. By the time I arrived, Tuskegee Institute offered a full academic college curriculum. Tuskegee was truly the "pride of the swift-growing South" not only by Coloreds but also by Whites. This pride was felt in Alabama, in all of the Deep South, and also in other parts of the country.

When Mother and I arrived on the campus, she told me to sit on the porch of Huntington Hall, a girls' dormitory, until she came back. She returned in about an hour after talking with the administrators about financial aid for my tuition. She had not told me that she did not have a penny of money to pay my fees. We were still in the Depression and Daddy had died two months earlier. However, this was not a deterrent to Mother; she was totally focused on my future. When she returned she said, "You are in but you will have to work." I was no stranger to work. After starting college, I realized very quickly that I was not in a minority of students who were working their full way through college on a "Five-Year Plan." I probably was on this plan during my first year there but did not know it.

In the earlier 1940s, there were still many sharecroppers in the Deep South. They wanted a college education for their children as much as anyone else did. It was a part of our culture that when the first child graduated from college, it was his or her responsibility to help the next sibling financially with college. There could be two or more children working their way through college. Many families were large and very poor and had as many as nine or more children; but this did not keep them from getting a college education. This practice existed in families other than sharecroppers', also, because we were all poor to some extent. The Institute also had students who did not have to work; they came from all over the country—the big cities "up North" and the Deep South.

Upon arriving at Tuskegee as freshmen, all students were required to be tested in Math and English Grammar. Students who failed were required to take remedial classes for the subjects failed. I passed both tests, although Math has always been my weakest subject. All students who had unsatisfactory grades after the first quarter were placed on probation for a specified time. If their grades didn't improve to a satisfactory level, they were dismissed from the college.

As I've already hinted, student labor operated the campus. They grew crops and raised livestock for food, cooked and served meals, worked in offices and the library, walked guard at night, worked in the school laundry, and performed other tasks. I was assigned to work in the school laundry. This was one of the hardest and most distasteful places to work. I stood eight hours a day, ironing on an ironing board. It caused calluses in my hands. I did this work from September to June of my freshman year. In the summer, I was assigned to even more distasteful work in the laundry: sorting the male students' dirty underwear. It must have been at least 100 degrees inside the building.

In my sophomore year, things started looking up for me in my work experience. I continued to work, but my new job was one of the most enjoyable and memorable experiences of my life. I was assigned to a job funded by one of President Roosevelt's New Deal programs, the National Youth Authority (NYA). I worked two to three nights a week and was able to attend classes in the day.

I accompanied an instructor to a rural area of Macon County, reminiscent of a Third World country. We went to what was probably a two-room schoolhouse. The students were adults. They had been instructed to save dried pine needles and dried corn shucks. The objective of these classes was to teach them to use these items to make useful articles for their homes. The instructor taught me to thread the loom with different colored threads. The pine needles were woven through these threads. A material was formed from which they made placemats, runners for dressing tables, and other useful items for the home. We also taught them to make baskets from pine needles and raffia. Basket-weaving was an art learned from American Indians who had lived in that area many years ago. The dried corn shucks were softened by soaking in water. The wet corn shucks were plaited and sewn together with twine and a special needle to form rugs of different sizes and shapes.

We also instructed the students to wash feed sacks with floral patterns and bring them to school. We brought dress patterns for children's dresses and taught the students to make garments for their daughters from the feed sacks. This was my first teaching experience. It was enjoyable because these adults were eager to learn. They also brought interesting life experiences to the table of learning.

There were three class periods at night. I attended the first and third periods even though I did not have any textbooks. My class for the third period was Biology. I went to the library to study during the second period, from books found there on the parts of the body that we were discussing in class. At the end of the quarter, in this large assembly class, approximately three students made C's, four made D's, and the remainder failed. I was one of the lucky ones to make a D. We heard the rumors that a male student in this class had a mental breakdown because he failed. We were also told that the instructor was fired.

Mother was able to send a little money toward my tuition for my sophomore year. It was very hard for her to do this. At the end of every quarter, money from home arrived late. One of my classmates, Gloria from Yazoo, Mississippi, and I would wait together in the lounge of our dormitory for the mail bearing our tuition. Gloria's mother was a teacher, also. Some of the girls living in our dormitory knew that Gloria and I did not have meal cards and could not go to the dining hall for supper. They would come back from the dining hall, tell us items on the menu, and ask us what we wanted them to bring us to eat. Such generosity by classmates happened to other students all over the campus.

I don't remember any socioeconomic distinctions on campus. Students helped each other. What I remember was bias in the selection of Miss Tuskegee, other queens, and for the best jobs on campus. These selections were primarily based on the color of students' complexions. Only very light-complexion students were chosen for "up-front"jobs such as in offices. We expected this as acceptable behavior. After all, this discrimination existed among some of our families and communities. These actions were an extension of what our ancestors had experienced during slavery.

However, this practice did not exist in our family. Grandmama had a very light complexion. Grandpapa was at the other end of the color spectrum with a very dark complexion. All of their children had an in-between complexion, except Aunt Addell, who was dark. She was loved as much as any of their children and was the favorite of Mimya, Grandpapa's mother. I remember Grandmama laughing hard when she told me how Mimya pronounced Aunt Addell's name: "Ah-ah-de-devil." She didn't speak English very well, and her voice was heavy with an African accent. This was the best way that she could say Aunt Addell's name.

Strict discipline and religion were as much a part of life at Tuskegee as they were at home. In the early days, there was a school on campus to train ministers. It was called Phelps Bible Training School. We attended chapel on Sunday mornings, Sunday nights, and Wednesday nights. This wasn't as bad as in the very early days when students went to chapel every night. On Sunday mornings we wore uniforms nicknamed "Booker T's" and marched to chapel accompanied by music from the school band.

Discipline was especially strict for girls at Tuskegee. We couldn't leave the campus without a written pass nor ride in cars with male students. We were advised by the Dean of Women that Tuskegee girls were "LAY-DEES" (ladies), as in the tradition of southern ladies. Nevertheless, we still had an enjoyable time in college. There were movies and dances in the gym on Saturday nights. "Star Dust"by Hoagy Carmichael was the lovers' anthem at the dances. Couples who were "significant others" always danced together to this song. We spent Sunday afternoons sitting on the many benches on the lawn. Sometimes, we went to Dr. George Washington Carver's Museum where he was seen often. Although he was advanced in age, he still worked in his laboratory where he had performed his world-famous experiments with sweet potatoes and peanuts. His work had aided in restoring the depleted land in the South.

My roommate and I also had another favorite thing to do. We would go to the tennis courts at every opportunity to watch the "fine" enlisted men of the Air Corps play. We didn't know anything about the game of tennis, but that didn't matter to us. We knew that they were in the all-Colored 99th Pursuit Squadron. We saw them studying in the library every night. They were part of the first class of thirteen in which all but five had "washed out," a term used for failing. We would hear about them washing out and wonder why. We knew that they studied very hard but did not know that there was a preconceived notion that Colored men could not learn to fly. Other outstanding men came into flight training in the fall of 1941. They were college graduates selected for pilot training only, not as future officers.

These men experienced segregation and considerable racism in that early class. Colonel Parrish, a White officer and native of Lexington, KY, came to Tuskegee later and did much to change the repressive and depressing situation that the squadron had endured. The 99th Pursuit Squadron, the 332nd Fighter Group, and the 477th Bombardment and Composite Groups will forever be known as the "Tuskegee Airmen."

They created a record of unmatched bravery in combat and for outstanding achievements in the European Theater during World War II.

One Sunday morning, December 7, 1941, my roommate and I came back to the dormitory from chapel to change from our uniforms into our "Sunday best" for dinner. We turned the radio on to listen to music. Instead of music we heard President Franklin D. Roosevelt informing the nation that the Japanese had bombed Pearl Harbor, adding those unforgettable words, "This is a day that will live in infamy." I remember us standing there in a state of shock, which quickly turned into anger. In January, men in their early twenties were drafted into the armed services for one year. There were many volunteers, also. The nation really didn't believe that the war was going to last very long. A popular song was written whose lyrics said, "Goodbye, dear, I'll be back in a year. Don't forget that I love you." That one year turned into several years.

CHAPTER 10
World War II

Near the end of the spring quarter of my sophomore year in college, I met a student from a suburb of Cincinnati named James Dillingham. We had dated for only a few weeks when I left college at the end of the quarter for summer vacation. I had no idea whether I would ever see him again. That summer, Mother was to attend school at Alabama State Teachers College (Alabama State University), a few miles from Tuskegee. Edgar and I had to go with her for those three months because we were still teenagers. James was still at Tuskegee and visited me often. That August, he asked me to marry him, after a three-month courtship.

We all knew that the war was deepening, not only by the news from the battle front but also by changes that we saw at home. A one-year conflict was totally out of the question. Men were being drafted at a faster pace and at younger ages; every man was expecting his "greeting" from the draft board. James had received his notice for induction. I learned later that James' mother had written a letter to Selective Service advising them that her son was a conscientious objector. As soon as this letter was received, he was drafted into the service.

Young doctors were also drafted, which left heavy patient loads on the doctors who remained at home and prevented them from making house calls. In fact, house calls by doctors have been largely extinct since WWII. I know because I gave birth to three sons during my marriage. My first two children were delivered by army doctors stationed in Fort McClellan. The third and last child was born after the war ended.

Cousin Leroy, who had gone to Detroit to live with his mother, my Aunt Willie Mae, when he was in his early teens, was drafted into the army from Detroit. Brother had gone to Detroit to work in the defense plants and was drafted from there in 1943. Edgar received his greetings as soon as he reached his eighteenth birthday. Just as everyone remembers momentous occasions in life, I will never forget the day that Edgar left for the service. Mother and I went with him to the Greyhound bus station. This is where he and other draftees caught an army bus that took them to the camp where they were to receive their basic training. It was a hot, sunny summer day. I was wearing a lavender maternity dress because I was pregnant with my second son.

Life as we had known it on the home front was changing, too. We were asked to make many sacrifices, but no one complained. We knew that everything we were asked to give up was for our enlisted men, and no sacrifice was too great. Food was rationed, which included meat and sugar. I learned to cooked tasty dishes from variety meats (liver, kidneys, tails, feet, etc.) They were available and were not rationed. Sometimes, we saw bright red meat in the stores' meat counters; it, too, was not rationed. I wouldn't buy it, though, because it was rumored to be horse meat. Aunt

Willie Mae sent part of her sugar ration stamps to me. Shoes and gasoline were rationed, too. The purchase of large appliances such as refrigerators, washers, stoves, etc. was almost impossible because the metals were being used to make ammunition and airplanes. Even mundane things such as chewing gum, cigarettes, and women's hosiery were hard to find.

There were large posters and billboards everywhere with Uncle Sam pointing a finger at us and admonishing that "a slip of the lip may sink a ship." We didn't know anything to say that would cause the enemy to sink a ship, but my peers and I learned from this experience that there are some things that people just don't repeat. (This art of keeping one's mouth shut has been lost on many people today.) We were also told that letters sent to servicemen were censored. Each enlisted man had an army post office (APO) number. I wrote my husband, James, so many letters that his APO number is still engraved on my brain 60 years later. Many women, who had never worked outside the home, went to work in defense plants. They were nicknamed "Rosie the Riveter."

We began to see flags in the windows of homes with one, two, three, or more blue stars on them. Each star represented a son in the service from that home. The saddest sight to see was a flag with gold stars. Each gold star represented a son who had died in the service. The most dreaded event was to get a knock on the door and find an officer of the armed services who had come to inform the family of the death of a loved one in service to our country.

Our close-knit family in Alabama was dwindling fast. In addition to the men in the family going into the service, the women were leaving to go north to work in the defense plants. Freddie, Aunt Addell's oldest child, was the first in her family to go to Detroit to work, in 1943. My Aunt Addell's husband was the next person to leave. He also worked in the defense plants. As soon as he found a place for them to live, his entire family moved there. Corine went to Detroit to work in the defense plant in 1943. Aunt Gertrude had left Anniston in 1937 when she married a widower who owned a business in the family's former home town of Clanton, Alabama. She continued to teach school there and gave birth to two daughters.

Mother took a civil service examination for the position of Army Recreational Director in 1943. She passed this examination and was assigned to a post in Stuttgart, Germany. While there for three years, she traveled all over Europe. After that tour of duty, she was assigned to other bases in the States. These included Fort Oglethorpe, Georgia; Camp Siebert, Alabama; Fort Rucker, Alabama; and the Charleston Port of Embarkation in Charleston, South Carolina. This experience of working for the armed services was the highlight of her life.

This exodus left Grandmama as the only member of our family still living in Anniston. Her daughters didn't want her to ever live alone. Therefore, after "Brother" went to Detroit, Aunt Addell sent one of her young sons to live with her. He was living with her in 1944 until he had to move with his family to Detroit.

Our Colored men went away to fight for our country with great patriotism, optimism, and hope. They were known by the labels "Colored" if they were from the South and "Negro" if they were from other parts of the country. These men came from all walks of life and had all levels of education. The only thing that they had in common was their race. One thing that they found in common in the armed services was the racist treatment that they received. The graduates of the ROTC college military-prep program had a hard time getting commissions. If a graduate did get a commission, he could not command White soldiers even if they were Privates.

It wasn't long before we were aware of this treatment of Colored/Negro soldiers. We knew of college graduates from Anniston who were not given duties other than those limited to service and support. Not all White officers wanted to be racist, but they knew that if they treated our men fairly they would be in danger from other Whites. This could include fights or demotion.

Our soldiers fought back in any way that they could, just as our ancestors did during slavery. One day I was in the Greyhound bus station in Anniston waiting for a bus to Greenville, South Carolina, where my husband was stationed. The waiting room was filled with Colored enlisted men. They told about their experiences in the service and spoke of "fragging." Fragging was an action in which a Colored soldier would fire a warning shot and sometimes a deadly shot at a racist White officer. This was usually done while on patrol at night. I learned later that "inside sources" informed the Chief of Intelligence Division, Colonel F.V. Fitzgerald, that Colored/Negro soldiers were hiding arms. Some of these soldiers admitted that they had guns and ammunition. Fortunately, many good changes were made in the military after the war ended. Since then, we have General Colin Powell (Ret.) and many other high-ranking officers of our race in the military.

1953

Mother as an Army Recreational Director –
World War II and the Korean War

Our enlisted men were disappointed that they were not allowed to fight. They did not want their duties limited to support and service. They wanted their contributions to be something more than loading and unloading ships, building airstrips, cooking, burying the dead, and other types of non-combat jobs. On the other hand, some men did not want to get too close to the frontline of fighting. However, their contributions did help to shorten the war.

This was especially true of the two all-Negro divisions that had been trained to fight in the infantry. These infantries were the 92nd and 93rd Divisions, which the War Department activated in 1942. There were about 18,000 men in each division. Some of the 93rd Division was stationed at Fort McClellan, Alabama, for basic training. This fort was located on the outskirts of Anniston. The 93rd Division landed in Guadalcanal in the South Pacific in January 1944. My brother-in-law was in this division but was discharged before they were sent overseas.

The 92nd Infantry came to Fort McClellan from Fort Huachuca, Arizona. They were known as the "Buffalos" because they wore an official shoulder patch with a black buffalo on it and an olive-drab background. They were organized in 1942 with the slogan "Deeds, not words." We Annistonians welcomed them into our hearts and homes. The night before they were to leave for overseas, they were confined to quarters due to a rumor that they had planned to destroy a segregated restaurant in the Colored business strip. This may have been just a rumor, but we believed it, perhaps wishfully, because we agreed with them that Blacks should not have been forced to enter and exit through separate doors in their own district. We will never forget the Buffalos for their great heart in fighting and for their

My brother in basic training – World War II

time spent in Anniston. They fought valiantly in the European Theater. Many lost their lives, many received Purple Hearts, and many returned home. These veterans returned to all of the racism that they had left and to the same segregated communities.

We received some news about the war and the battles that were being fought even though we lacked the technology that we have today. We were not as inundated with news of WWII as we would be in future wars. During WWII, we received our information via radio and newspaper. If something of great importance occurred, an extra edition of the newspaper would be printed quickly. Men would stand on street corners with papers, shouting, "Extra, extra! Read all about it!" followed by the appropriate headline. We knew about the Japanese suicide bombers. They would dive- bomb, or "Kamikaze," their planes into allied naval vessels and kill thousands of enlisted men. We also knew about all of the great battles that were fought, such as the landing of allied forces on the beaches at Normandy and those fought in the jungles of Iwo Jima.

I am sure that many Americans were glad that the war was not fought in our country. We knew about the air raids in Great Britain and France—the news was frightening. We were especially disturbed by the treatments of our POWs in both theaters of action. It seemed that treatment by Japanese soldiers was more barbaric than that by the Germans. We were proud of our enlisted men, that no matter what transpired, they gave only their names, ranks, and serial numbers.

Although Colored/Negro servicemen experienced racism everywhere they served during the war, some good things came out of the experience. They learned about different cultures, which made them more appreciative of being American and less accepting of racism at home. Deep, lifelong friendships developed between soldiers of different races. After all, who cares about the color or race of a man who is in the same foxhole with you?

Edgar didn't have good experiences in the service, either. He buried the dead all of the years that we fought in the European Theater. When that part of the war was won, he was sent to the South Pacific to do the same thing again. There were about 1,500 Americans to be buried and nearly 23,000 Japanese who also had to be buried. I asked Edgar, "Why were you sent to the South Pacific to do the same job that you had done in Europe?" He replied, "They SAID that they had lost my papers." It was a horrific experience that caused him to have nightmares for at least two years after he returned from the service.

World War II was finally over in 1945. It seemed that we went straight into the Korean War, where our enlisted men also fought valiantly. Fortunately, the men in our family came home safely. Brother returned to Detroit, where he fell in love and married. He and his wife were together for many years before she preceded him in death. Leroy also returned to Detroit. However, he was a very changed person emotionally and, perhaps, mentally. I now know that he may have been suffering from Post-Traumatic Stress Syndrome. I did not have a chance to see him again after he left Anniston because he lived only a few years after the war, but I will always remember him as my fun-loving cousin who was very protective of me.

Although our men did not have the best experiences during the war, we know that there is some good in everything bad that happens. Among the good things that came out of WWII was the integration of the armed services by President Truman and the G.I. Bill of Rights. Through this Bill, men who had dropped out of high school during the Depression had a chance to return to school and receive a diploma. This Bill also paid college tuition and provided an opportunity for the veterans to purchase homes. Edgar took advantage of all of these opportunities. He finished high school and graduated from Alabama State University. He majored in Biological Sciences as pre-med. Although he didn't have the opportunity to attend medical school, he never lost his love for Medicine. He taught Physical Science and surgical assistance in the Cleveland public school system.

Something else wonderful happened to Edgar, which wasn't realized until 30 years later. He was living in Cleveland, Ohio, and receiving his health care from the Cleveland Clinic. One day, when he was about 60 years old, he called me. He had just returned from an appointment at the Clinic, where a neurologist had examined him and asked him whether he had ever had a learning disability. Edgar didn't remember the difficulty in learning that he'd had as a child, but I did and relayed this information to him. Maybe the shock of his war-time experiences played a part in his improved learning ability later. After he graduated from college, he couldn't get enough of learning and was always taking additional college courses. I finally told him that he should be taking courses leading to an advanced degree. He took my advice and received a master's degree in Education Administration and Counseling.

Corine, the other person in our little childhood gang, left Detroit in 1948 to live in California and ultimately retired as a teacher from the California public school system. She received a Baccalaureate Degree from California State

University. She also met the love of her life in California and remained there for 46 years before moving to Texas.

CHAPTER 11
My Marriage: Rainy Days, Dark Nights

James and I had one of those whirlwind WWII marriages that were very common. Some of these marriages lasted, but many did not. I did not have a wedding, but the ladies who lived in the neighborhood brought flowers from their gardens to decorate the landlady's living room for the ceremony. James and I were married by Rev. Ralph Riley, pastor of the Dexter Avenue Baptist Church, Montgomery, in August 1942. This church would be pastored by Dr. Martin Luther King, Jr. in later years. Dr. King named one of his sons Dexter, for this church.

This particular August was also the time when Mother received her Bachelor of Arts degree. She had persevered for over 20 years after graduating from junior college to reach her goal of becoming a college graduate. She was a very focused and determined person. I learned from her example that we never get too old to learn or have our dreams come true.

The day after our wedding, James and I took the train to Cincinnati, where he was to be inducted into the service. After we paid for the train tickets, we had fifteen cents left. During those twelve-plus hours of train ride, we had just enough money to buy a small box of cheese Tid-Bits as our only source of food. We arrived in Cincinnati at 3 a.m. James used the leftover nickel to call his uncle, who lived downtown near the Union Station. His uncle came to the station and took us to his home. His uncle asked, "Is there anything that I can get for you?" I answered quickly, "Some food, please." I had never been so hungry in my life. He and his wife cooked bacon and eggs for us.

After we finished eating, we were taken to his parents' home. They lived on a quiet street. The modest homes on this street were owned by blue-collar workers. When we arrived, I did not know that his family had no knowledge of our marriage. I had assumed, because my mother and family knew about our marriage, that James had told his family, also. This situation and its obvious lack of communication was an early signal that we were both too young to marry. I was 18 years old, very naïve and trusting. James was 20 and very immature—how immature, I would learn through the years. He had one sibling, a brother, who treated me as if I were his sister. His father was a kind and gentle man. He loved his sons, unconditionally. He also loved the Cincinnati Reds. When both of his sons were in the military, he felt guilty when he went to see the Reds play instead of going to church on Sunday. He donated blood to the Red Cross as frequently as he was allowed. This was his contribution to the war effort.

My mother-in-law hated me from the moment that she met me. She always thought that I was the reason for James not graduating from college. What she did not know, and I also did not know until after the marriage, was that he had been kicked out of Tuskegee University the year before I arrived. He had told me that he was majoring in tailoring. In reality, he was taking a course in aero-mechanics on the campus, and it was not part of the college. His brother and I learned the truth, but we let his mother go to her grave without knowing what really happened to her son.

James visited with his family for two weeks before leaving for basic training. I was to stay with his family until he could send for me. Three awful months passed before he sent for me. It should be no surprise that I left as soon as possible.

I went to as many places as I could and lived in some terrible conditions to be with James while he was in the service for two and a half years stateside. We never did get sent overseas. The longest span of time that we were in one place during the war was in the second year of our marriage. This was when James was stationed at McDill Field in Tampa, Florida. We lived in Ybor City, a Cuban community. It was about one-half block from the Cuban Plaza, an open-air pavilion with a covered bandstand. I could hear the music, mostly Hispanic, from my bedroom window. Big bands were also featured, such as Count Basie and Jimmy Lunceford. When these big bands were there, I would take my only child with me to hear the music. He was just beginning to talk and was learning to speak Spanish from hearing it spoken. Surprisingly, some Cubans had a darker complexion than I. Often, I was mistaken as Cuban and was spoken to in Spanish. I would smile and say, "Si-Si" without knowing what had been said to me. I enjoyed Cuban food, the best of which was the Cuban sandwich. You haven't really eaten a good sandwich until you've eaten one of these.

My Children (L-R) James, Jr., 13;
Edgar, 12, Gerald, 9 years of age

When James was discharged from the service, we came back to Ohio to live. His parents rented to us an apartment on the second floor of their home. There, my life became a living hell. His mother set out to break up the marriage and she succeeded. During that period I learned that he was a mama's boy. He had no backbone and was also a heavy drinker. I thought that if I could get him away from his mother, maybe we could make a go of it. We moved to two different places in or near the city, but it was still too close. It didn't work.

During the first year of my marriage, certain incidents occurred that were red flags signifying that this marriage was not going to be good. Over the next several years, my marriage became the most emotionally and verbally abusive situation imaginable. Through it all, I discovered the truth that children are very perceptive of unhappiness in a family. One of my sons, who was only five years old, started chewing the ends of his collars. Knowing that to be an abnormal behavior, I took him to Children's Hospital for a complete physical examination. Afterward, the doctor said that my son was in good health and asked, "Are you in a happy marriage?" I answered, "No." He said, "Well, your son knows this."

I was trying hard to stay in the marriage for my three sons' sake. However, I was beginning to suffer both physically and mentally. I had a headache every day. I took an over-the-counter medication, called Stanback, for the pain. It all made me feel as though my head had left my body and was spinning around the room. The worst part of this situation was the recurring nightmare that I experienced for many years. In this nightmare, I would be falling from an airplane, plummeting through the pitch-black darkness of the night—falling, falling, falling. Finally, the nightmare changed. On that night, I was in the middle of the ocean. It was pitch-black again and I was drowning. I was going down for the third time when I awakened suddenly. I was probably close to a mental breakdown.

Finally, James added physical abuse to the verbal and emotional abuse. I knew then that I had to leave, which was what he and his mother wanted. My mother-in-law told him to send me and the children back down South. She also told him that when I crossed the Ohio River, he would not have to give me a penny of money. The day that I left he said, "You have been the best wife a man could ever have." I replied, "I won't be this good to another man." He said, "Yes, you will because it's the only way you know to be." It was true of my Southern culture; we had been taught to treat our men with great favor.

It was a long time before I could understand why I had been treated so terribly. James had not been forced to marry me; the decision to marry was mutual. Years later, I realized that in addition to all of his faults, he also had low self-esteem. This gave him the need to destroy my self-esteem, and did he ever!!! Psychology teaches that when a person with low self-esteem feels less than you, he has to bring your self-esteem down to his level by destroying it. This process is called leveling. When I left James, my self-esteem hadn't just been leveled—it had dipped to minus zero.

I believe that there are faults on both sides of a failed marriage. My fault was possibly being too passive. I couldn't say anything to my mother-in-law about the chaos that she was creating in my marriage because I had been taught to respect my elders. Growing up, I hadn't been told anything about relationships; therefore, I had no tools with which to work. In fact, I hadn't been told much about anything such as sex or changes that would occur in my body during puberty. I grew up in what is known as the "Silent Generation." Mother did the best she could in that era with what she knew to do, so I don't blame her for anything.

With that terrible marriage behind me, one would have thought that better times were coming. However, the really hard part of my life was just beginning. In 1950, I went home to Alabama with my children and had no idea that I would not be welcome. Mother was no longer working for the armed services or anywhere else. Grandmama and Edgar were also living there. I got a job working for a Colored businessman who had an enterprise that operated on a 24-hour-per-day schedule, with two twelve-hour shifts. A relative of the owner, "Little Bob," was the day-to-day manager. I worked a twelve-hour shift for two weeks, which then reversed to a twelve-hour night shift—all for $10 a week. We were so unaware of business methods that we didn't realize this company should have had three shifts operating. However, we were very glad to have any kind of job. In addition, we had been taught that we should always support and be a credit to our race.

I was so overwhelmed by everything that was going on in my life that I lost 25 pounds almost overnight. Grandmama did the best she could to help me with the children, but Mother gave me absolutely no support. Quite a few people in my little hometown were very nice to me when I was down and out. I will never forget their kindness. These were working-class people who were truly the "salt of the earth."

Mother didn't ask me what had happened in my

marriage or how I had been treated, and I did not tell her because we simply did not have that kind of relationship. In hindsight, I believe that she thought I should go back to my husband. But I did tell Grandmama the cruelties that I had experienced because I knew that she loved me unconditionally. When I finished telling her all of this, she was furious and uttered the first and only bad words that I ever heard her say: "If I were you, before I'd go back to that man, I would eat bread and drink piss." I asked Grandmama why I had such a hard time in life. She said, "God gives each of us a cross to bear. Some people's crosses are heavier than others. It is a test of your faith." (At that time I didn't know anything about how heavy the cross was that she was bearing—that her family had been run out of Georgia and everything taken from them.) I never forgot her words concerning a test of faith. I have had many, many heavy crosses to bear in my life, but I have always known that God would be there to help me.

At the end of the first year after I left James, I was about to experience the most painful time in my life. Grandmama came to me one day without warning to tell me that she was going to Detroit to live with Aunt Willie Mae. She said, "You must let me take the older children to their father because your mother doesn't want me or those children here." I started crying and said, "I don't want my children to leave." She replied, "Don't cry. Those boys will come back to you when they are older." When she said this, I am sure that she and Aunt Willie Mae had discussed at length what they thought was best for me. Like them, I couldn't see any other way out. My salary of $10 per week wouldn't pay for food, rent, and a babysitter for three children. I cried for days. That event was so painful that I can't remember when or how the children left. It is a memory that has been blocked from my mind.

During the next year, we learned that Aunt Gertrude was seriously ill. She could no longer work or care for her daughters. Mother took her to Detroit to stay with Aunt Willie Mae and Grandmama. The family hoped that she would receive better medical treatment there. However, this was not to happen because she was determined to be terminally ill. Aunt Gertrude died in 1957 while her daughters were teenagers. Family was always important to us and became a special time to bond in caring for her daughters. The girls lived with Mother in Georgia until they graduated from high school.

After graduation, the oldest girl went to California to live with Corine. She worked days, went to school at night, and graduated from Redlands College. She is married and still living in California. The youngest girl went to Detroit to live with Aunt Willie Mae. She married and raised a family there and still lives there.

CHAPTER 12
Second Chance

During the second year after Grandmama left, I had more and more trouble tolerating Little Bob's abusive treatment at work. Running amok with his authority, the most despicable thing that he did was to try to trick me into stealing money. One of my duties was to account for money that went into the main part of the company. Knowing both that I was totally dependent on this job and that I was having a hard time financially, he decided that I was an easy target. "Little Bob" had the books audited and found them to be correct. This was a big disappointment for him. Because I didn't steal, he tried something different. One day he put an extra five dollars into the receipts of that day, which was half the amount that I made per week. I pointed out the discrepancy to him; again, he was disappointed in my honesty. That was the last straw—I couldn't take anymore. I told him in so many words to "take this job and shove it" and walked off the job, not knowing from where my next meal would come.

I went downtown the next day and got a job running an elevator in our only hotel. There, I made one dollar less per week and worked only eight hours a day on a five-day shift. I worked there for only a short while because after paying a babysitter I had only six dollars left. I worked anywhere that I could to make a little more money. At a movie theater I helped with the cleaning, sold tickets, and alternated selling concessions there at night. I also worked many other nickel-and-dime jobs in order to make an honest living. Although these were mundane jobs, I did my best. When I informed my employers that I was leaving, they always said, "Mary, if you need a job and I have an opening, I would be happy to hire you again."

Many years later, I went back to Anniston for a visit. I told my friends there that I especially wanted to see one person, "Little Bob." I wanted him to see that I had become successful in spite of his meanness. They said, "You don't need to see "Little Bob" because God has already taken care of him for you." With that, they took me to see the shack where he had lived before he went to stay in a nursing home. That's when I remembered hearing our elders say, "God don't love ugly" when someone did something wrong. Believe me, He really doesn't.

In my efforts to make a better living soon after I'd left "Little Bob's" company, I started working as a nurse's aide at Anniston Memorial Hospital. I was assigned to the Obstetrical and Gynecology (OB-GYN) floor. This would be one of the greatest blessings that would be bestowed on me. Mrs. Benson, the head nurse on this floor, was one of the nicest women I have met. There were three Colored aides; the rest were White. Mrs. Benson treated all employees equally. In addition, she became my mentor. She brought her OB-GYN nursing textbooks for me to read. When there was a difficult delivery, she had me scrub, mask, and gown and go into the delivery room to observe. There also were occasions when she took me to the labor room to feel the baby's movements in the birth canal or to "special" (sit with) pre-eclampsia patients. Pre-eclampsia patients had hypertension; they could have gone into convulsions and possibly coma.

In that environment, I began to feel good about myself. My work at this hospital was definitely a life-changing experience. My supervisor had no idea what she had done for me. This southern White woman had helped me to regain my self-esteem. I began to think that perhaps I could do more than this. Although I had been out of school for ten years, I started thinking about going back to college and decided that I wanted to be a registered nurse who delivered babies. I had no idea until the Seventies that nurses in the baby-delivering profession were designated as certified nurse midwives.

With my goal set, I applied to the Grady Hospital School of Nursing in Atlanta. I was told that I would need $300 to enter and would be able to work in the hospital to cover the remainder of my fees and living expenses. At that time, it was as hard for me to get $300 dollars as it would be for me to get $3 million today. In addition, I didn't know who would keep my youngest son; I had no money to pay a babysitter.

Evidently, someone told Mother of my efforts to go back to school. One day, she came to me and said that she and Edgar would pay my college expenses if I wanted to return. I was unaware then that she had accepted another tour of duty as an Army Recreational Director, stationed at Camp Rucker, Alabama. While there, Mother met her second husband, Mr. Herron. He was a civilian barber on the post. After they married, they came to Columbus,

Georgia, where she accepted a teaching position at Spencer High School. Her husband worked as a civilian barber at Fort Benning. Unfortunately, Mother was in her new marriage for only a few years. One morning, she found Mr. Herron dead on the front steps of their home.

I applied for admission to the School of Nursing at Tuskegee University in the summer of 1952. I also requested work for that summer because I wanted to make the financial situation as easy as possible for Mother and Edgar. Soon, I received news from Tuskegee: I was accepted to the college and was given work. I was also allowed to live in the nurses' dormitory, which was new and very nice. However, all of the news wasn't good. When I talked to the Dean of the School of Nursing, she told me that I would have to start as a freshman instead of as a junior. The truth was that my first two years in college had been spent primarily in working, not in attending classes.

Disappointed but not deterred, I was not ready to give up the opportunity to work with patients. I studied the Tuskegee bulletin to see what my options were. Also, I had decided that if I had to continue in Home Economics, I wanted to graduate with my class in 1954. In order to do this, I would have to take ten additional courses that had been added to the curriculum during the preceding ten years.

Before I started taking classes, I had a lucky encounter with a graduating senior on campus during the summer. Undergraduates would usually ask graduates what they planned to do after graduation. This student told me that she was going to get her A.D.A. I asked her what that meant. She said that she was going to do a one-year dietetic internship in an approved hospital, become a member of the American Dietetic Association (ADA), and work as a hospital dietitian. I had not heard of hospital dietetics at my separate but unequal high school, so I asked her what I would need to do to get into a dietetic internship. She gave me the name, address, and telephone number of a Colored dietitian who worked at the predominantly Colored veteran's hospital in Tuskegee. That dietitian lived in Greenwood, a middle-class neighborhood near the campus. I made arrangements with her to visit her home and talk.

One of a few students on campus who owned a car took me to this dietitian's home and stayed with me during the meeting. I learned that there was a core of subjects that I would need to take in order to be considered for an internship. These courses needed to be added to the additional courses that I would need to graduate with my class. Included were several extra courses in chemistry, other sciences, and nutrition-related subjects.

Once again, I did not give up. When I went to register for the fall quarter, I asked for permission to take extra courses. This request was denied. I was told that my grade point average (GPA) from the first two years in college wasn't high enough to allow me to take the extra courses. When I registered for the second quarter, I asked again to take extra courses. The Dean of Students said, "You were told last quarter that your GPA wasn't high enough." I showed him my grade report from the previous quarter. He was amazed because I had made all A's. I was able to do better in my classes this time because I had textbooks rather than library books, I didn't have to work, and I was more highly motivated at the age of 28 than I had been as a teenager in college. Although I was taking more than 20 hours each quarter, I made about three B's; the rest of my grades were A's during my last two years in college.

In addition, I was classified as an adult student. Many of the male students were WWII veterans and my peers. I had several platonic friends among these veterans, who looked out for me in many ways. Other good things happened to me, also. One day, when I returned to my dormitory from class, I heard girls chatting in the room across the hall. One said, "Dilly, you are being rushed." I asked, "What does that mean?" She said, "Look on your bed." I looked and saw a note written in red ink on beautiful ivory parchment paper. It was an invitation from Delta Sigma Theta sorority. They were inviting me to attend a rush party at the Faculty Cottage. I felt honored because I was an older student, sort of like Sally Field when she received an Oscar and said, "You like me, you really like me." In addition, Delta Sigma Theta was considered a very prestigious sorority. Other fine sororities allowed prospective pledges to write letters requesting consideration for their sororities, whereas Delta Sigma Theta did not. I made it through probation and was inducted into a true sisterhood.

Some of our instructors were really great. Not only were they gifted academically, they also taught life strategies that would endure with us. One professor who made a tremendous impression on me was the instructor who taught Philosophy of Education. He was also the Dean of the School of Education.

Unfortunately, a few athletes in his class didn't make their best effort. On one occasion, we were assigned to write a term paper. When we received our graded papers, one of the basketball players asked me about my grade. I told him that I had made an A. I asked him, "What did you make?" He replied, "An F minus." I said, "Oh, no one makes an F minus." That evening, he came to my table in the library and said, "Dilly, I want you to see my term paper." I looked at it and saw that he really had made an F minus. The next day, I learned something very important from this professor. When those athletes complained about the difficulty of the assignments, he replied in a stern voice, "What do you want me to do—crack a hole in your head and pour the information in?" He meant that students shouldn't study just to pass tests. Instead, students need to put what they learn into the computer of their brains for future reference. Fortunately, there were also other great instructors of this caliber at Tuskegee University.

I graduated cum laude with my class in 1954. I also received three honor awards. Each student who was interested in receiving appointment to internship could apply to only three programs. We applied early in our senior year. Although I didn't have all of my core subjects completed, I applied to an all-Colored internship on the East Coast, Tuskegee's Dietetic Internship Program that would open in the fall, and Boston's Beth Israel (Beth Israel Deaconess) Hospital. We waited with great anticipation for a certain date in April to know whether we were accepted and to which of the three internships. I had applied to the two Colored internships because I thought that I would have a better chance.

I was accepted as an alternate at the East Coast hospital but was not accepted at Tuskegee's internship. However, I was accepted at the Beth Israel Deaconess Hospital. I went to Mrs. Powell, Dean of the School of Home Economics, to ask why I had not been accepted at Tuskegee. The only reason I had applied to Beth Israel was on her advice; I had not previously heard of this hospital. She explained that they wanted me to go where I would measure against students from other parts of the country; translated, that meant how I would perform with White students. What she really wanted for me was to get out of an all-Colored environment. I didn't realize what a wonderful thing she had done for me until I started working in my profession. This was another great blessing that I received career-wise. I was accepted to this dietetic internship and was able to complete the rest of my core subjects during the summer sessions.

I entered my internship in the fall of the same year. In our class of ten, I was joined by another Colored student, two Jewish, one Chinese, and five White. The hospital gave our class a welcome party that was a lot of fun. In the midst of it when I was talking, I became aware of a deep silence in the room and became quiet. They said, "Don't stop talking—we love your Southern accent." This set the pace for the remainder of the year. I wasn't treated as an inferior, as being stupid, or as someone who had just stepped off the banana boat simply because I was from the South. Five of us in the class did a lot of fun things together. We were one Jewish, a Chinese, one of French descent, a native Bostonian who was a devout Catholic, a New Englander, and me. We had good times together, although we worked extremely hard.

There was another first experience for me that year: The Women's Auxiliary of the hospital gave our class tickets to attend a theater performance. I truly enjoyed my first experience of live theater and was hooked for life.

I don't believe that I could have had a finer clinical experience at any other hospital in this country than at the Beth Israel Deaconess. There were two other dietetic internships in Boston: Peter Bent Brigham and

Massachusetts General Hospital. We had our classes together but did our practical work in our individual hospitals. We traveled by bus, subway, or train to our classes.

Boston was truly a medical Mecca. We had our first class at the Harvard University School of Public Health. It was taught by the Dean of the School of Public Health. The subject for that class was Malnutrition. Our class on the diabetic diet was taught by a dietitian on the staff of Boston City Hospital who had worked with the committee that developed the diabetic exchange system. At that time, this system had been in use for only about five years. All of our classes were of this quality.

Another rewarding experience that we had was in weekly dietetic rounds for our class. A doctor took us on rounds to meet selected patients and to learn both their diets and their diagnoses. After we had seen the patients, he took us to a conference room. There, he would then go into greater detail about the diagnoses and the relationship of the diet to each particular disease. We absolutely loved these rounds and attended them even on our days off.

On the other hand, the administration part of our internship left a lot to be desired. Some of this shortcoming was compensated by our six-week administrative affiliation at Massachusetts General Hospital.

Booker T. Washington said, "The older I grow, the more I am convinced that there is no education which one can get from costly apparatus to which can be gotten from contact with great men and women." I agree. Louise Hatch, the Director of Dietetics at Massachusetts General

Hospital, was one of these great women. She received the Copher Award from the American Dietetic Association in 1976. This award was established in 1945 for outstanding accomplishments in the profession of dietetics.

My rotation at this hospital occurred toward the end of the year and near graduation. We had started sending resumes and applications to hospitals. I asked Miss Hatch how hard it would be for me to get a job. She said, "Just decide what you want to do and where you want to work, and then apply." My fear of racial discrimination influenced my decision of where to apply. Based on this fear, I applied to a Jewish hospital and a veteran's hospital, both in Ohio. I also applied for a teaching position at Meharry Medical College in Tennessee. I wanted to teach Nutrition and Diet Therapy there. When Mrs. Reiner, the director of dietetic internship at our hospital, learned that I had applied for a teaching position at Meharry Medical College she was very pleased. She made arrangements for me to teach Diet Therapy to medical students from Tufts University, Boston. Our class had also taught Diet Therapy to the medical students from Harvard University. I taught the students from Tufts alone.

Miss Hatch's prediction proved to be correct. I was offered positions at each of the places to which I had applied. The Jewish hospital telegraphed an offer for an administrative position. However, an administrative position would have defeated my purpose for entering dietetics; I would have had very little opportunity to be with patients. Meharry offered me the position of director of dietetics at the hospital where the medical students received their experience with patients. Because I had just completed my internship, I did not think that I had enough experience to handle this type of position. So, I asked Miss Hatch whether she thought that I could handle it. She answered, "Just remember, it all starts with the menu." I never forgot those words. She didn't mean taste, appearance, texture and nutrition; these factors are understood as the basis for good menu planning. What she was referring to was the need to consider budget, available equipment, number of employees, and time required for preparation. I added her comments to my list and considered my options.

CHAPTER 13
My Career

I chose the position at a veteran's hospital in Southwest Ohio, believing that there certainly would not be discrimination at an institution of the federal government. When I interviewed, I was offered a position as a clinical dietitian. This offer pleased me very much. However, I was puzzled by the last words that the director of dietetics said to me: "I want you to wear a clean uniform every day." I wondered why she said this. I wasn't dirty; I was wearing a dress that had just been dry cleaned. To me, her statement indicated racism and disrespect for me as a person.

To clarify, I didn't leave the South because I hated it. I still love the South because this is who I am. Instead, I came "up North" believing the "bill of goods" that we had been sold in the South, that everything would be equal here. However, I found that things were only slightly better. Our men were called "boy," just as they were in the South. We could use public accommodations but in a racist sort of way: There were invisible "Colored only" and "White only" signs in many places. Negroes here knew where those signs were and obeyed them. The racism here was covert, whereas in the South, with visible signs, it was overt. A White woman here in Ohio described racism in the South as traditional and racism in northern states as pure hate. She was so right.

I still believed that I would be treated fairly in the federal system until an incident occurred in my third year there. A position became open for an administrative dietitian. I was asked to fill in at this position, which I did for a year, without extra pay. Although administrative work wasn't my choice, it paid more and I needed more money because I was a single parent. When I started working there, the beginning salary for dietitians was $3,610 annually—the most money I had ever made, but still not much. When this position was finally filled, it was given to a White dietitian who was already on staff. My supervisor asked me to help her, which I tried to do diplomatically. I don't think that I had been voted as the most diplomatic woman in my college's senior class without having had some knowledge and skill in using diplomacy. But this dietitian was very resentful of my efforts to help her.

I was hurt very deeply by these events because I hadn't thought that this could happen here. The hurt turned to anger and then to hate for Whites for about three days. The emotion of hate made me feel sick—I had to get over it. I still thought that perhaps a mistake had been made, so I went to Personnel. I inquired as to why my work was good enough to keep me in this position for a year but not good enough for me to be hired and paid to fill the job permanently. I was given an unbelievable explanation: the White dietitian, even though she had not performed that job, (supposedly) ranked one-tenth of a point higher than I.

However, as a result of my visit to Personnel, fliers were posted all over the V.A. center, stating, "It is against federal regulations for an employee to be kept in a higher position for more than 90 days without awarding that position to that employee or filling that position with another employee." In hindsight, I don't think that it had ever occurred to them to consider me for this position; they simply had never had a Negro dietitian in an administrative position.

All things considered, I had to get away from that general medical and surgical hospital (GM&S), but I couldn't afford to quit my job. Therefore, I asked to be transferred to a 120-bed geriatric hospital on the grounds of the same medical center, which was thought of as just a place where veterans who needed assistance were sent to die. Although most of these patients didn't leave the hospital, they were treated with a lot of love and care. There had never been a dietitian at this hospital. Dietary had been run by a Food Service supervisor who had done a good job based on what she knew to do. I decided to take this lemon that had been given to me and make lemonade. My work at this geriatric hospital turned out to be one of the highlights of my career.

When I had been there for only a few days, I could see that some changes needed to be made. A key issue was my noticing that the employees were racing to use the restroom after serving breakfast and cleaning the kitchen before setting up and serving lunch. It didn't take a rocket scientist to see that something was wrong with that picture. I felt that the only way I could learn what was going on was to work both employee shifts in one day. The employees were told of my plans. They were assured that whatever I would note would benefit them, as well as the patients.

I observed the layout of the equipment and voiced my recommendations to my supervisor that improvements could be made in this area and for serving meals to the patients. This meant that the food that was prepared at the GM&S hospital and arrived hot would be served hot to all patients. Additionally, I recommended work-simplification methods in the serving line and received permission from the directors of dietetics and nursing to make these changes, which worked beautifully. The director of dietetics came over to see the changes and was very pleased. She said, "Mrs. Dillingham, surely God will have an extra star in your crown for the work you have done with these patients." Next, arrangements were made for me to present a program on geriatrics to our local dietetic association. Speakers, which included a physician, a registered nurse, a physical therapist and me, presented a panel discussion on these various aspects of geriatrics.

Furthermore, a geriatrician (a physician specializing in geriatrics) came in twice a week for rounds with the medical staff and patients. The two physicians and the two head nurses who were on staff, the Chief of Physical Rehabilitation, and a corrective therapist participated in these rounds. I also attended the rounds when I could. The director of dietetics still wanted me to work at the GM&S hospital part-time. The doctor who was chief of the medical service at this hospital told my director that they were very pleased with my work. He informed her that the specialist had requested that I be scheduled so that I could attend all rounds. My schedule was changed, and I learned a great deal on those rounds.

Some time later, the dietitian who had been given the promotion instead of me at the GM&S hospital asked for a lateral transfer to a different position. Thus, the administrative dietitian position was posted again. This time, I received the promotion.

My only real problem in that position was that some of the White dietitians under my supervision resented having me as a supervisor. An older White dietitian had an especially resentful attitude. A younger White dietitian asked me how I could stand that woman's treatment. The day did come when I had taken all that I could. I went to my supervisor and told her how I had been treated. She said that she would talk to our director when she returned from vacation. That night, the resentful dietitian called my home and asked me not to tell our director how she had treated me. I told her that I wouldn't tell, under one condition: I expected from her the same respect that she would give to a White dietitian in my position. She said she would and became my greatest ally. Once again, I was able to see some good in something bad that had happened to me. The experience I had acquired while working in this position without extra pay had taught me nearly everything that I came to know about administration and more than made up for what I didn't learn in my internship.

One day in August 1963, while working at this hospital, I noticed that the employees, one by one, were leaving their work stations for a few minutes. I thought it was odd that so many employees had to go to the restroom. Finally, the last employee returned and said, "Mrs. Dillingham, you should have heard him. He said, 'I have a dream.'" She went on to repeat verbatim what she had heard. That was when I realized that the employees had gone to hear parts of Dr. Martin Luther King, Jr.'s "I have a dream" speech. I finally had the opportunity to hear this great speech in its entirety on television.

This incident reminded me of a day when I was a student at Tuskegee University. One afternoon, I was on my way to class and noticed students running across campus to chapel. This was unusual because these were not normal chapel hours. I asked someone what was happening and was told that Thurgood Marshall was speaking there. At that time, he was an attorney for the NAACP. He became the first Black justice of the Supreme Court. The Civil Rights Movement had started in the South during the Fifties. During this time, we decided that we no longer wanted to be identified by the labels "Colored" and "Negro" that slave owners and others had given to us. We were now Black and/or Afro-Americans who were proud of our color and ancestry.

When my youngest son graduated from high school and enlisted in the Navy in 1964, I decided that I was in the position to make some changes in my life. I wanted to go to Cleveland, where my brother Edgar was living. So, I put my little house up for sale and gave a six-month notice of my resignation. I accepted a position in a private hospital in Cleveland and stayed there for only two months because the racism was excruciating for me and the dietary department was run so poorly. When the employees learned that I was leaving, one of the Food Service supervisors came to me and said, "Mrs. Dillingham, you are the tenth dietitian to quit this year." On my last day of work there, I was asked to go to Personnel for an exit interview. The representative in Personnel said to me in a voice filled with exasperation, "Tell us what is wrong with that dietary department." I minced no words in telling her. At that time, in spite of this experience, I found Cleveland to be more liberal than any other major city in which I had lived in Ohio.

After that exit interview, I called the Personnel office at the V.A. hospital in Cleveland and was hired right away. This hospital had been opened for about three years, and they were still trying to get organized. They had moved from a hospital that had an entirely different food-delivery system. This new hospital had a state-of-the-art, centralized food-delivery system versus the old decentralized system. However, my impression was that they had dramatically underestimated the number of employees needed for this new system. Dietitians were still working the same shifts as other employees. In many instances, they were performing the duties of food-service employees on a regular basis.

After I was there for about six months, the Chief of Clinical Services of the dietary department resigned. I was asked to take this position. Although it would be a two-grade promotion, I declined on the basis that it was an administrative position. After receiving assurances that the position was all clinical, I accepted the promotion. This position turned out to be both administrative and clinical. The administrative changes that I made in patient clinical service were another highlight of my career. These changes made the administrative aspect of the clinical service more manageable.

What I enjoyed and am most proud of is the work that I did with the dietetic interns there. This internship program was very similar to the one from which I had graduated in that three hospitals were included with their separate programs. They were the V.A., Mt. Sinai, and University hospitals. All of the students did their academic work at Case Western Reserve University. The major difference was that at the end of the year each student received a master's degree in addition to becoming a member of the American Dietetic Association.

In my position as Chief of Clinical Service, I developed and evaluated the clinical experiences for our interns. I did the same for interns from the other two hospitals, who chose an emphasis in clinical dietetics and did an affiliation at our hospital. Frances Fischer was the faculty member at Case Western who coordinated the academic studies and hospital affiliation for all interns. Once again, I was blessed to have the opportunity to work with one of the great women in our profession. This Miss Fischer received the Copher Award in 1979.

One of the most rewarding experiences that I had in my career was the opportunity to see, after graduation, former dietetic interns whom I had taught. One such occasion occurred at a national convention of the American Dietetic Association in Washington, DC. Former students and I were happy to see each other again. Each said that she was employed in a high-level position in the field of nutrition and dietetics. They told me how much they appreciated my efforts in their training. I was so proud of them.

At a similar meeting in Las Vegas, I saw one of the clinical dietitians who had worked under my supervision in Cleveland. She had been looking for me and was about to resort to leaving a message for me on the message board. When I asked about her employment, she said, "I am working with the Women, Infant and Children (WIC) Program in Texas." When I asked, "Which city in Texas?" she replied, "I am in charge of the WIC Program for the state of Texas." I exclaimed, "The whole state!" You can't imagine my pride when she said, "You were my mentor."

She felt this way because I had recognized her potential and tried to keep her challenged. I had assigned her to more complicated areas such as the renal dialysis unit and to a patient who was on a special research diet. One day I told her that she should think about working toward an advanced degree. She took my advice and received a master's degree from Case Western Reserve University.

I attended as many state and national dietetic conventions as my finances would allow. Time from work always was given without financial assistance. During the thirty years that I worked, I had my expenses paid to only one of those meetings. That was during the last year that I worked and was given for my assistance in recruiting someone to fill my position. I have no hard feelings about this situation because I attended meetings to learn more about my profession. Continuing hours of education were not required at that time. I never forgot the kind advice that one of the staff dietitians at Beth Israel Hospital gave to me. She said, "Learn all you can. It will be like money in the bank. It will be yours, and no one can take it away from you." I never forgot those wise words and always lived by them.

Working with students on this level brought about another life-changing decision for me. When they had come to me they were like blank sheets of paper. But by the end of the year, I realized that they knew more than I did. I didn't like this feeling. For this reason, I enrolled in the Graduate School of Nutrition at Case Western the next year. I took one of the most enjoyable courses, World Nutrition, at night and made an A. The Dean of the School of Nutrition asked me to come back the next semester. I declined because I had to work too hard both on my job during the day and to attend school at night. However, my experience in this class made me think seriously about getting a master's degree. I never forgot that I had been offered a full scholarship to pursue a master's degree in Education at Tuskegee University. However, I had declined this offer because of my desire to work in hospital dietetics. Over the years, after graduating from college, I took classes at night in preparation for writing a master's thesis if the opportunity would ever arise.

I really wanted to attend Case Western Reserve University full time. But no matter how I did the math, I just didn't have the money. I didn't give up, though. I thought about state universities where fees for state residents are much lower than those at private universities. With this in mind, I submitted an application to the Graduate School of Medical Dietetics at the Ohio State University (OSU).

Weeks turned into months as I waited to hear from OSU. The long delay in receiving a reply to my application could have been due to the director not being apprised by her staff. Or, ignoring my application could have been based on fear due to race riots in Cleveland that had resulted in the National Guard patrolling the V.A. hospital grounds. However, I was not deterred. I called the registrar's office every week. I knew that I had excellent grades and had been a resident of Ohio for many years; therefore, they had no legitimate reason not to accept me. Finally, the registrar's staff grew tired of my calling and told me that I would have to call the director of the School of Medical Dietetics, Martha Nelson Lewis, because it was out of their hands. I believed that when Mrs. Lewis would meet me, she would realize that she had nothing to fear.

I received a Master's degree from
The Ohio State University in 1969

I talked with Mrs. Lewis by phone and was asked to go to Columbus for an interview. Although she was very nice, I don't remember talking with her for more than five minutes. At the end of our talk, she said that I was accepted to her department and that I would receive a letter of confirmation within a week. Edgar and I decided to look for an apartment for me while there. After reviewing a copy of "The Lantern," the OSU school paper, we went to an apartment building that was new. The staff there told us that all other apartments were rented except the one in the basement; I soon learned that this was not true. However, the basement apartment was very nice for me; it was quiet and had a private entrance.

The next week, as promised, I received a letter confirming my acceptance to OSU. Much to my delight and surprise, the letter also stated that I had been awarded a grant that would pay my tuition for 18 months of graduate study. In addition, a stipend was included to pay for other expenses.

Mrs. Lewis was, perhaps, the most well-known recipient of the Copher Award. She established the first coordinated undergraduate program (CUP) in dietetics in this country. This is a program in which a student completes four years of college studies in nutrition and dietetics. These studies are integrated with clinical and administrative experience in a hospital. As a result, the student receives membership in the American Dietetic Association in four years instead of five. Fifty CUP programs exist today.

My time at OSU was a very volatile period all over the country. Many Civil Rights leaders had been assassinated, including Medgar Evers and Malcom X. The assassination of President Kennedy grieved the entire nation. I doubt that anyone who was alive at that time has forgotten where they were when they heard the news of his death. I am proud that I had had the opportunity to hear and see him when he spoke on the courthouse steps in downtown Dayton, Ohio. People stood shoulder to shoulder the width and length of the street in front of the courthouse as far as he could be heard over the public-address system. I still remember the little dog that accompanied a student from the University of Dayton. The dog's back bore a placard that stated, "I wish I was a people so I could vote for Kennedy." I was grateful that I could vote for Kennedy because I had come from a time and a place in which Blacks hadn't been permitted to vote.

Although Mrs. Lewis was very fair, racism was alive and well on the campus of OSU. It seemed that all of the closet bigots had come crawling out from under the rocks. I was there from 1967-1969, which probably was the most tumultuous time of the Civil Rights Movement. There were disturbing images on television of Afro-Americans demonstrating peacefully who were hosed down with fire hoses. Police dogs were also turned on them. When Dr. Martin Luther King, Jr. was assassinated in 1968, Blacks all over the USA were saddened and enraged. Riots erupted, and it seemed that all of America was on fire. That summer, Bobby Kennedy, the president's brother, also was assassinated. Despite the turmoil during this period, a great achievement occurred in our country: Man walked on the Moon for the first time. When we looked up at the Moon, we found it hard to imagine that man could walk on this bright shining object, so far away.

Overall, life at OSU proceeded well. I was very fortunate that the major professor for our nutrition courses was as fair as Mrs. Lewis. I liked the way she taught. Her method of teaching reminded me of the method used by the dean of the School of Education at Tuskegee University. She didn't spoon-feed us. There were times when I left her class and went directly to the School of Agriculture library to do further research on the topic of the class that day. Sometimes, I would stop by her office after leaving the library with further questions. Additionally, I had a fantastic professor for Physiological Chemistry. Mrs. Lewis asked me to audit this course. This background knowledge was crucial in my understanding of our major courses in nutrition, which was taught at the cellular level. I wasn't aware until the second year that we were taking these classes with doctoral-level students. Especially gratifying, as a graduate teaching assistant, was my receiving a letter of commendation for teaching Personnel Administration in the undergraduate medical dietetics program.

After receiving my master's degree, I had no problem finding a job—I was accepted everywhere I applied. The best job offer that I had was at the State level of Cooperative Extension of Ohio with a faculty appointment at OSU. However, I did not take this position, for personal reasons. I also had other reasons for not taking other positions that were offered to me. After remaining on the faculty at OSU in the Medical Dietetics Department as a lecturer for two quarters, I decided to accept the position of Director of the Dietetic Internship at Montreal General Hospital in Canada.

One of my goals for pursuing an advanced degree had been to become a director of a dietetic internship. I had enjoyed my work with the dietetic interns in Cleveland very much. I also liked the arrangement of this program in Montreal because it was similar to the one from which I had graduated and had affiliations with other area hospitals' dietetic internships.

I fell in love with Montreal when I attended Expo '67 (a world's fair) there. It was a beautiful, clean city with friendly people. I had met the director of dietetics of Montreal General Hospital while attending the national convention of the American Dietetic Association in Boston. At that time, I had no thoughts or intentions of living or working in Canada; nor had I decided to pursue an advanced degree. After deciding to go to Canada, I applied for my landing papers, which is similar to having a green card to work in the U.S. It took about four months to be processed through Canada's immigration department. This process included going to Chicago to meet with immigration authorities. I took a morning flight from Columbus, Ohio, and a return flight on the same day.

After I arrived in Montreal, I rented a third-floor walk-up apartment. The best thing about this apartment was the location. It was within walking distance of the hospital and only two blocks from the Metro (subway). I rode the bus to work because there were steep hills to climb. I walked home every day regardless of the temperature, which was minus zero degrees for many consecutive months. I didn't mind the cold, although I seemed to be in a minority of persons not wearing fur. Men, women, and children wore fur coats. Fifty inches of snow wasn't uncommon, but they had excellent snow-removal services. I came to the conclusion that there were two seasons there, winter and July, which is how citizens of Montreal describe their own climate.

One of the main streets, St. Catherine, was also within walking distance of my apartment. When the weather was nice, I would go there on Saturday mornings to walk and "people watch." "People watching" was fascinating there. Although I enjoyed Montreal, I didn't forget home and always bought the Sunday edition of the "New York Times." I met one dietitian who was also from the States. I went to many places alone on the Metro. The stations were well-lighted and safe, and easy-to-follow directions were posted everywhere. The walls were covered with beautiful mosaic tile. I went to see Bill Cosby at the Performing Arts Center, although I had seen him perform twice in Las Vegas.

My supervisor was one of the nicest people I have ever met. She did everything she could to make my life, off the job, enjoyable. She invited me to have dinner with her and her friends at very upscale restaurants. She took me to see the performances of two ballet companies and to the opera. She also took her mother and me to a flower show and to see the tulips in bloom at Parliament in Ottawa, Ontario - the capital city of Canada. This was a wonderful sight to behold. The tulips were spread like a beautiful, multicolored blanket across the grounds. My supervisor told me that the queen of Holland had donated to Canada the bulbs for the tulips.

Montreal is perhaps the largest city outside of France with as heavy a French influence. I joined the Quebec Dietetic and Canadian Dietetic Associations and attended all of the meetings of the Quebec Dietetic Association in Montreal. The most memorable meeting that I attended was at Notre Dame Hospital. Everything written in this hospital was in French—all signs, all notices, everything!

Not only that, every word spoken in the meeting was in French. Attendees who didn't speak French were given earphones that carried the English translation. I felt that I was in a meeting of the United Nations.

I have always thought that French is the most beautiful foreign language. It has such a graceful and lyrical sound. I tried to learn French before I ever thought about going to Canada. In Cleveland, I took a class in French at night but didn't do well. I even bought French-language records and tried to teach myself, to no avail. In Montreal, I took a French class at night. I learned to read French fairly well but could not understand the spoken word.

However, one day my efforts paid off when I attended the National Restaurant Association meeting in downtown Montreal. All writing in the building was in French. I was able to read the sign that stated the time (3 p.m.) and location for a cooking demonstration! As we entered the room, we were given a small copy of the recipe to be prepared. The dish was Quiche Lorraine, and the recipe was written in French. As the chef began the demonstration, he narrated in French. With that came an undercurrent of mumbling throughout the room. I asked the man sitting next to me what was the problem. He said, "We don't understand a word that he is saying." You can't imagine my joy. I understood every word and realized that I was not really so dense, after all. My French teacher was from France, and he had taught us French as it is spoken in France. I enjoyed all of my experiences in the cosmopolitan city of Montreal.

CHAPTER 14
The Last Stop

I decided to come back to the States after spending a year in Canada. Fortunately, I was able to obtain a position as a teacher in an inner-city high school in Dayton, Ohio, in 1970. I had applied for this position shortly before I left Canada. When I arrived in this city, I went to the Board of Education to ask about the outcome of my application. They told me, regretfully, that they were looking for someone who was certified to teach Vocational Home Economics. Puzzled, I asked, "What is that?" When the four areas of this specialty were explained, a light bulb went off in my head. The areas were Food, Clothing, Child Development, and Home Management. These areas were the exact content of one of my majors in college. The core courses that I had taken to be eligible for a dietetic internship gave me a double major of Vocational Home Economics and Nutrition & Dietetics. In my work experience, I had used only my major in Nutrition; the fact that I was certified to teach Vocational Home Economics had been completely forgotten.

All teachers of Vocational Home Economics in the state were required to attend a three-week workshop at

Miami University before school opened. We were told not only about making lesson plans but also what the administration expected from us as teachers and what we were to expect from our students. Students were to provide copies of their birth certificates and to open savings accounts at a bank. Teachers were to find jobs for them in the subject areas that we taught and to visit each child's home. We also were instructed to visit the students' jobs while they were at work and to ask their supervisors about their performance.

I was assigned to teach Foods and Child Development. Very little cooking was done in class. I believed that these students needed to know more about foods that they would not ordinarily know from their life experiences. They needed to aspire to do more than flip hamburgers by being exposed to other areas of food service. There is nothing wrong with flipping hamburgers; it is honest work. I simply wanted them to do better. I had a difficult time getting jobs for them in the food industry. During my conversation with proprietors of food establishments, they promised to call me in a few days but did not call. When I called again, they would not go to the telephone to talk with me.

The proprietor of a very nice restaurant located downtown agreed to give my students a tour of his business as a field trip. It was very informative not only for the students but also for me. In addition, he allowed them to have lunch free of charge while we were there. After the students chose their food, waitresses took their trays to the table. One student said, "Mrs. Dillingham, we have never had anyone take our trays for us." It was a good experience for everyone.

The V.A. hospital did provide jobs in the dietary department, where students gained good experience in quantity food preparation and service. The best way for the students to get their required hours of work was to work on Saturdays. Therefore, I went to the hospital on Saturdays to check on them.

When I thought about teaching Child Development, I was somewhat anxious. I had taught it as part of my Directed Teaching experience but had not thought about this area of my education since my days at Tuskegee University many years earlier. I could only hope that I would recall this knowledge as readily as I can recall how to ride a bicycle, and I did. I remembered that my instructor had advised me to have the gynecologist from John A. Andrew Hospital speak to my students about the use of contraceptives and the practice of abstinence. My instructor explained that the families of these students were extremely poor and everyone usually slept in one room. It was impossible for these girls not to be aware of their parents' sexual relationship and not to conclude that such activities were acceptable for them.

In my new assignment to teach Child Development, I didn't go so far as to teach my students about contraceptives and abstinence. When I remembered my original teaching experience, I realized how amazing it was that we had done that in the 1950s, when there was no epidemic of teenage pregnancies. The lesson that I had learned from that experience was to teach at the level that I found the student. This concept also had been emphasized by our instructor of Home Economics Education at Tuskegee University, Bennie Mae Ware-Rankin. Bennie Mae, as we called her out of her presence, was both revered and feared.

When she taught, she spoke to us in a firm, measured, no-nonsense voice. An example that she used for this concept was related to meeting the students at their socioeconomic level. For example, she said, "The students may not have sheets to sleep between. Teach them to sleep between CLEAN whatever they have."

I didn't have any trouble getting jobs for my students in Child Development. They worked in daycare centers in the inner city. Fortunately, I also was able to reach back to other courses from college, such as Art, as well as Child Development, to teach them to think creatively in planning learning experiences for the daycare children. I taught them to make useful items for children from articles that usually are thrown away. To my mind, another lesson on conservation is always worthwhile.

In college, my instructor in Directed Teaching had taken me on a home visit to a house that was in a very rural area of Macon County, Alabama. The road we traveled was so deeply rutted that I was afraid an axle would break on the car. Because of this experience in college, I wasn't surprised when we were asked to make home visits in my new assignment. Having a small class, I was able to visit the home of each of my students except one. Extending the same respect that they would give to their pastors, my students' parents graciously welcomed me into their homes and had a good rapport with me, thanks to prior telephone conversations about concerns for their children.

A very unusual occasion came as a result of these visits. One morning as I was teaching, the assistant principal escorted a parent to my classroom. He probably thought she had come to chastise me about her child. To the contrary, she was returning the visit that I had paid to her home. She was dressed as nicely as she would to attend church, including a hat. I will always cherish the memory of that visit because it meant so much to me.

Learning truly is a two-way exchange. My students and I taught one another a great deal. I believe that they knew I cared about them and did my best.

However, my education and work experience weren't being utilized fully. For this reason, I applied for other positions as a dietitian/nutritionist. My desire was always to work with patients but in better working conditions than I had experienced in hospitals. In May, I was asked to interview for a position at the Montgomery County Health Department in Dayton. During the interview I was offered a position as a staff nutritionist, which I accepted. Once again, I was fortunate to have a supervisor who had a strong educational background in Public Health. She had a master's degree in Public Health Nutrition from the University of California at Berkley. My entrance into Public Health was with little knowledge of this area of health care; but the intense orientation that I was given alleviated some of this lack. My belief is that many citizens of any city do not realize the scope of the good work done by their health department.

Shortly after I started work there, my supervisor resigned. I was offered the position of Supervisor of the Bureau of Nutrition, which I accepted. My supervisor in 1971 was very supportive. The Director of Nurses at that time also was supportive. She made it very clear that she wasn't my supervisor but that I would work closely with the nurses. She also told me that the chief of nutrition for public health at the state level wasn't my supervisor, either. However, she provided good advice when she suggested that I write a letter to the chief of nutrition in order to introduce myself. She also advised me to include in this letter my short-term and long-term goals for the Bureau of Nutrition. This letter was highly instrumental in establishing good rapport for me with the chief at the state level for years to come.

The health commissioner requested that I recruit an Afro-American dietitian/nutritionist to fill the position that I previously held. My recruitment began at Tuskegee University. A young lady was recommended who was a recent graduate of the college and its dietetic internship. She was not only qualified but also very capable. She was hired as my assistant, and I gave her the same intense orientation that I had received.

Together, we set up nutrition-education components in well-child and prenatal clinics. Unfortunately, we received a lot of resistance from the nurses who had always provided this education. The mothers in well-child clinics were sent to us after their babies had received their immunizations. The babies were crying; the mothers were anxious to get home and in no mood to talk with us. In order to change that situation, I requested assistance from the nurse who was in charge of all of the clinics. The nurses finally gave in. Their behavior had been a simple matter of resisting change, but we ended up working well together. We had excellent support from the beginning when we set up a nutrition component in prenatal clinics. We established nutrition components in the East Dayton and West Dayton (Charles A. Drew) Health Centers. The doctor in charge of the East Dayton Health Center included in his budget a paid position for a dietitian.

I was on "cloud nine" whenever I was asked to make home visits alone or with registered nurses. This gave me the opportunity to use my clinical knowledge and to be creative in challenging situations. Instructions to bake or broil food could not be given to someone who had only a hot plate or an oven that didn't work. A way also had to be innovated to instruct the use of a half cup of ingredients to someone who had no measuring cup. These patients were low-income, but they were often very concerned about what to do for the welfare of their family members. Unfortunately, some health care providers lumped these types of patients into the "same box" of not doing what they were told to do. As a result, in giving instructions they did not meet the patients on their level of understanding.

During my first few years there, I taught classes in nutrition at each nursing substation. For fifteen years, Public Health experiences were planned and evaluated for the ten dietetic interns each year from the major teaching hospital, Miami Valley Hospital, in our city. As time went by, experiences in Public Health were provided to any master's degree-level graduate who requested them as part of a program to become a registered dietitian. Occasionally, this experience was requested for students in the graduate program of nutrition at Case Western Reserve University in Cleveland. During that period, I also taught Community Nutrition part time at the University of Dayton for several years.

I never forgot that my salary was paid by public funds. Therefore, I felt a responsibility to be involved in any area in the community that had some relation to nutrition. I was on several advisory committees in various agencies.

I believe that my most valuable contributions were to advisory committees of the Nutrition Program for the Elderly, Cooperative Extension and the Miami Valley Child Development Centers. Nutrition lectures were given when requested, sometimes at night. As the results of a grant proposal that I wrote, the health department received State funds for a nutrition-education project for the elderly, which included a position for a dietitian/nutritionist.

One day in 1974, I received a call from a sales representative of Ross Laboratories in Columbus. Similac baby formula is one of their products. He invited me to a meeting in Dayton. A new program in nutrition, to be established by the government, was discussed. Representatives from Children's Hospital and anti-poverty agencies also attended. The project was described in which free food would be given to low-income pregnant women and infants and to children up to five years of age. It was what became our present-day Women, Infants and Children (WIC) program. I thought the idea was fantastic! Young women were interviewed in prenatal clinics who previously had confided during dietary interviews that they had sold their blood to buy food. Their confessions not only helped to stimulate the program's creation but also activated my vivid memories of being pregnant with my first child and the days when a bowl of oatmeal and an orange were all I had to eat. It wasn't difficult for me to realize the need for this program in the Health Department. I discussed the idea with my supervisor and gladly received his permission to try to acquire this program.

When the time came to write the grant proposals, I was very grateful that I had been selected a few years earlier to attend a workshop at the University of Minnesota, where I had learned the basics for writing grant proposals. I was one of several Public Health nutritionists chosen from across the State of Ohio and the country to attend this weeklong workshop. Our grant proposals for the WIC Program in Ohio were submitted to the regional office of the United States Department of Agriculture (USDA) in Chicago, after they were submitted, the Chief of Public Health Nutrition for Ohio called to inform me that my grant proposal was one of the first received and was very impressive.

My proposal was accepted and chosen as one of 20 programs in the U.S. to participate in a research study that was conducted during the first year. As part of the study, we sent blood work and other data to the Triangle Research Center at the University of North Carolina in Chapel Hill. That first year, we had only 50 infants in our WIC Program. By the time I retired, there were 3,500 women, infants, and children participating in our WIC Program. Today, as I write, Montgomery County's WIC Program has approximately 12,000 participants.

I retired from the Health Department in 1987. The 15 years that I worked there were some of the most enjoyable years of my career. The only blight on my time there was resentment from most of the White dietitians, as coordinators of the WIC Program, for having to accept supervision from me. One particular dietitian was especially virulent in her resentment toward me. She tried to convince everyone that I was incompetent. My first and only experience like this was in my first position as a hospital dietitian. That was 25 years earlier. Some things change, but many stay the same. However, the chief of

Public Health Nutrition for Ohio came to my retirement luncheon and set the record straight. In addition, I received a plaque for my work in training dietitians/nutritionists and a certificate of appreciation from the Senior Citizens Center of Dayton. I was blessed to receive or be offered a promotion in every position in which I worked.

CHAPTER 15
A Test of Faith

My retirement has been truly enjoyable. I attribute this to some years of careful planning. It goes without saying that we have to plan financially. Being a child of the Depression, planning wasn't hard for me to do. I have never lived up to my means, as my favorite talk show hostess said before she became very wealthy. We also need to plan for our physical well-being. This means having a healthy lifestyle, beginning years before we age, and developing interests and activities that will sustain us both before and as we grow older.

I also attribute my enjoyment in retirement to having had my mother as a role model. It has been said that a child's greatest role model is the same-sex parent. This was truer for me than I had realized as a younger woman. Mother retired as a teacher at Spencer High School in Columbus, Georgia. I remember wondering what I could give her as a retirement gift and recalled a watercolor painting that she had done and hung on the dining room wall in our home in Anniston. Thinking that she would enjoy painting in her retirement, I gave her a correspondence course in oil painting, called the

Famous Artists Painting Course. Like Mother, when I retired, I took painting classes for several years and enjoyed painting in my retirement.

I bought a small house as a retirement home. Mother had done the same thing. An avid gardener, she grew vegetables in her retirement; I grew flowers. She also loved to travel. So, when I retired, I, too, traveled extensively—around the world, in fact. What follow are some of the things that I have done and seen in my travels.

In Japan I rode the Bullet Train. In China, I walked the Great Wall, saw the Terra Cotta Warriors in Xian, and walked on Tiananmen Square. I "shopped till I dropped" in Hong Kong, drank Singapore Slings in the courtyard of the Raffles Hotel in Singapore, and saw the native wood carvers at work in Bangkok, Thailand. My trip to the Far East was my most enjoyable. Additionally, I listened to the symphony orchestra in the Sydney Opera House and saw some of the most beautiful fish swimming around the Great Barrier Reef in Australia. I also visited all of the ancient ruins in Athens and cruised the Greek Islands. Like the rest of the world, the U.S. has many wonderful places to visit, the most beautiful of which, in my opinion, was northern Arizona around Sedona and the Grand Canyon. Every vista, in my own country and others, brought joy to my heart.

Like Mother, I, too, have drawn satisfaction in volunteer work during retirement. Mother was active in the Retired Teachers Club, in her church, and in activities with children. I, too, have been active in the church and was a volunteer with the area Literacy Council. Helping others, whenever possible and at any age, is important.

My brother living in Cleveland, Ohio in 1973

Mother died in 1976 at the age of 79. She was blessed to be sick for only a few days. Most of her family had preceded her in death. Grandmama died in 1962 at the age of 86. She was still living with Aunt Willie Mae in Detroit where another daughter, Aunt Addell and her family, was living. Her greatest joy was to live in Detroit where her only son, "Brother" (my uncle), lived. He was the joy and love of her life, and everyone knew it. Grandmama was alert to the end of her life. One night she said, "I will place my clothes on the foot of the bed where I can reach them easily in the morning." She died peacefully in her sleep that night. Six years later, her daughter Leona died. Brother and Aunt Addell died in 1985. Like Grandmama, Brother died in his sleep. He and Grandmama were two of the sweetest and kindest people who ever lived. Perhaps, they were what all people should be like, as described in the Sermon on the Mount: "Blessed are the pure in heart, for they shall see God."

The most devastating death in the family for me was the death of my brother, Edgar, at the age of 65. I experienced more overwhelming grief at his death than I did at my mother's or Grandmama's death. I had never thought of Edgar and me not being here for each other. We always had been so close that we could feel each other's pain hundreds of miles apart.

For example, I had a strong urge to call him on one Saturday night. This was very unusual because I never called on Saturday. He was divorced and could have been out or had company in his home; so, I was not alarmed when he didn't answer his telephone. I called again on Sunday afternoon, when we usually talked. Still, he didn't answer. I thought that perhaps he had gone to a movie because, as adults, we still enjoyed movies as much as we had as children. When he still didn't answer that evening, I began to become alarmed. After the telephone operator checked for trouble on the line and found none, I told her my concerns. She offered to have the police to check his home, but I reluctantly refused. The next day, one of Edgar's friends called from Cleveland to tell me that he was in intensive care in a hospital. After he recovered, he told me that he had heard the telephone ring that Saturday night but had been too sick to answer.

A similar incident happened to Edgar. He called me on a Friday night and asked whether I was okay. I had been to the dentist that afternoon for a badly abcessed tooth. The dentist told me that I hadn't arrived a minute too soon. When I told Edgar what had happened, he said, "I called you because I thought I heard you calling me from the other room in my house. I heard you so clearly, I went to that room to see if you were there."

When Edgar passed, I was depressed for so long that my sons became very concerned about me. They knew how much I loved to travel and suggested that I take a trip. However, it was words from an unexpected source that comforted me in my grief. Those words came from my attorney when I went to his office to have Edgar taken out of my will. He said to me, "As we grow older, we start losing our family and friends." I had never thought about that before, but those words have sustained me as I've grown older and lost more and more family and friends.

My favorite aunt was Aunt Willie Mae. Members of our family in Detroit brought her, now nearly 85 years of age, to Edgar's funeral. Although she still lived alone, kept house, and looked fine, I felt strongly that something wasn't right with her. For this reason, I called my cousin in California. I told her my idea that the family in Detroit should do something nice for Aunt Willie Mae for Christmas and that I believed it would be Aunt Willie Mae's last Christmas with us. The family in Detroit accepted my suggestion, gave her nice gifts, and took her out to brunch. Then, I called her on Valentine's Day, as usual. When I asked about her health, she gave me her usual upbeat answer but then changed her mind and told me that a tumor had been found in her lungs. She hadn't been diagnosed as having a problem before Christmas, but I somehow had sensed an issue with her health. Our bodies speak to us, and she, knowing that something was wrong, had transferred her feeling of uneasiness to me so that I, too, knew that something was wrong with her. She didn't suffer long and died that spring.

I had another great loss in my life, too. After several years as a single person, I had met my second husband, Richard Herald, a chemical engineer. We came from similar backgrounds and had a lot in common. Unfortunately, we did not have many years together before his death. I had hoped that we would grow old together, but he died of a massive heart attack at the age of only 56. I believe that my brother and late husband are guardian angels watching over me.

In our lifetime each of us encounters valleys and peaks. We have our good times and our bad times. My faith has been tested to its utmost. As a health care provider for over 30 years, I took care of my own health as much as I could. I always self-examined my breasts every month, had my doctor examine them, and a mammogram was performed every year. On doing my breast exam one month, I felt a lump. I told myself that it couldn't be cancer and went on a cruise that was already planned. However, the discovery of that lump was in the back of my mind. I dreamed about it during the cruise.

On returning, I went to my family doctor. He sent me to a surgeon, who arranged for me to have a biopsy in the next few days. The result of the biopsy was negative. I learned, however, that this surgeon had left most of the lump in my breast. Six months later, I found a large lump under the armpit on the side where the biopsy had been done. I went back to the surgeon, who removed the lump. He said casually, "You have infection somewhere in your body." I asked whether part of the remaining lump could become malignant. He said, "Not that I know of." Another six months later, the lump had grown larger. I returned to my family doctor. He wanted me to go to the same surgeon again, but I refused and asked to be referred to a different surgeon.

The new surgeon examined my breast and said something about making flaps. I knew that he was talking about doing reconstructive surgery. I replied, "I don't want to hear anything about flaps," because I didn't believe that I had cancer. He must have thought I was crazy. He did a lumpectomy (removed the lump) with wide margins around the tumor, then drew a diagram to show me what he had done. I really appreciated this visual explanation. On the first office visit to the surgeon after surgery, he said, "You have breast cancer." I said, "I don't believe it! I want to see the pathology report." There, on the pathology report, was the diagnosis, as big as life: "Papillary carcinoma." He told me that I had a form of cancer that had a high recurrence rate. Although I appreciated his honesty, I left his office in a daze and a state of shock. The "Queen of Denial" was my title for about a week until reality set in. The fear that washed over me was like what I imagine it would feel like to have the barrel of a loaded gun pressed against my head or a big Mack truck run over me.

The surgeon sent me to a radiation oncologist. He examined me and said that the cancer hadn't spread. This gave me some hope. He also told me that he would always be honest with me. His promise meant a lot to me. I did some reading on my type of cancer and learned of a 50-percent possibility of a recurrence. My belief in the power of positive thinking led me to place myself in the 50 percent of patients who would NOT experience a recurrence.

As a very private person, I told no one about my bout with cancer except my family and my best friend. I knew that these people would honor my request to keep this knowledge to themselves. The main reason was my desire not to see "skulls and crossbones" in the eyes of others. I knew that cancer was no longer an automatic death sentence and wanted positive attitudes to surround me. My life experiences had taught me that prayer works and changes things. I called members of my family all over the country and asked them to have their churches pray for me. At that time, I belonged to the International Federation of Christian Living. This group was also asked to pray for me. Then, I prayed for myself a prayer that went from the soles of my feet to my heart and straight up to God, who reached down and touched me. When I put myself in the hands of God, I felt strong and had no fear.

My treatment involved 30 sessions of radiation in addition to medication for the next five years. I drove myself to the hospital for each treatment and was always the only Black patient in the waiting room. It wasn't hard to see that cancer is an equal-opportunity disease that doesn't care anything about color, creed, age, or sex.

At the end of the first year after my bout with cancer, I realized that I had experienced a spiritual renewal—a closeness to God that I had never felt before. I also realized that I have a sixth sense that allows me to see through people and situations that relate to me. I consider this ability, as a result of my cancer, to be a gift.

My doctors observed me very closely for eight years after surgery for cancer. I also did my part with monthly self-examinations of my breasts and annual mammograms. After these years, my doctor believed that my annual mammogram looked suspicious, although he had felt nothing on the physical exam of my breasts. After a second mammogram was done, a needle biopsy was scheduled for me and performed in about fifteen minutes. A band-aid was placed on the area where the needles had been inserted. The biopsy was positive for cancer, and surgery was scheduled for a mastectomy.

I had no fear this time. My insurance gave me 32 hours for surgery and hospitalization. My surgeon, who had done the first surgery, gave me a prescription for pain medication when I was dismissed from the hospital. I didn't take any of those pills because I had very little pain. Instead, I took only three or four over-the-counter, maximum-strength pain pills. At my first office visit one week after surgery, my surgeon said, "In all my years of practice, I have never had a patient come in to see me one week after major surgery in such good condition." He also said that the doctors did not expect a recurrence of this cancer.

When I told my dentist about the small amount of pain I had had following breast-cancer surgery, he pooh-poohed it. Then, I repeated what my surgeon had said on my first office visit after surgery. The dentist replied, "Well, you know why." I didn't say anything because I really didn't know why. However, I decided that I would try to find the reason. The Book of Psalms has always given me answers to my questions and comfort to my heart. So, I read the Book of Psalms that night until I found the answer in the forty-first Psalm that God will take our pain unto Himself in certain circumstances.

Although I am a very private person, I wanted in some way, without saying that I had overcome cancer, to tell how faith had brought me through. I tried to do this in a Bible study group, but no one wanted to hear it. I felt bad about this reaction until I read an article in a religious tract by an author who had had a similar experience. No one had wanted to hear about her faith, either. So, she decided that instead of trying to tell people about how her faith had sustained her, she would just live her faith. Like her, this is what I decided to do. This decision has brought me a wonderful sense of peace and much happiness.

"There is great gain in godliness with contentment." (I Timothy 6:6)

I have been free of cancer for more than five years since my last surgery. As a two-time cancer survivor, I can't say enough about the value of early diagnosis, which saved my life. I also owe a lot to good medical care and, above all, to God.

CHAPTER 16
And I Say

I am in the sunset years of my life. Most of my close relatives and friends have passed on. Of those of us who were close in childhood, Corine and I are the only leaves left fluttering on that branch of the family tree. I have seen a lot of changes in the world during my lifetime. Some of these changes have been good, and some haven't been good. I believe that the most significant changes have been made in Medicine and health care. We are living longer and have better lives because of these changes.

One great improvement is that we have inoculations for communicable diseases of childhood. When I was a child there were red quarantine signs on homes of children with whooping cough. It was frightening to hear little children coughing so hard that it seemed they would cough their insides out. Another is that we don't see signs of rickets in extreme bow legs anymore because our foods have been enriched with vitamin D. Also, polio was a dreaded crippling disease that struck children primarily. It was called infantile paralysis. I remember that as a pledgee to my sorority, part of my probation activities was to read to children stricken with polio, at John A. Andrews Hospital.

I was not prepared for what I would see: little ones in wheelchairs as far as I could see down the corridor. It was a sight that I will never forget. Today, we have a vaccine for polio.

Tuberculosis (TB) was the AIDS of my day. There was no stigma attached to TB, though, just great fear of contracting it. Conversely, the misplaced stigma of AIDS has been carried too far. Perhaps, if the presence of this disease in my race hadn't been "swept under the rug" there wouldn't be as much of it present today among us. It is a self-perpetuating form of genocide in the Black race. As for TB, there was no cure then, just as there is no cure of AIDS today. The only thing that we knew to do was to give patients lots of nourishing food and fresh air. There is a cure for TB today, and I believe there will eventually be a cure for AIDS.

Thankfully, we have many antibiotics to control infections today. Although penicillin was discovered in 1928, it wasn't widely used until 1940, including for a particularly virulent and transmittable type of infection known as venereal disease. When I was a child there were billboards along the highways stating, "STAMP OUT VENEREAL DISEASE." We learned more about the use of penicillin during WWII; it was used to save the lives of thousands of GIs. It also was used to cure venereal disease in men so that they could be inducted into the armed services. Today, it is used widely for many types of infections. Also, many tests and other methods have been developed for the early detection of numerous types of cancer.

One of the new endeavors in Medicine today is research that may yield a cure for many diseases for which no cure currently exists. It has become a political issue, but it has great promise. Before we go too far into this effort, sufficiently strong safeguards and ethical standards should be established to deter anyone from making money illegally. There will always be someone somewhere who will try to find a way to make money illegally from something. I place the science of cloning animals as one of the new things that is particularly frightening because there are scientists who want to clone humans. I remember hearing Daddy say, "When man gets to the place where he thinks that he can make another man, we will be near the end of time." That was in the 1930s, and his words make me wonder today.

With all of these advances in Medicine, it is very disheartening to know that more Afro-Americans die from nearly every disease than other races. This discrepancy is due to a lack of information and access to health care. Afro-Americans have been stereotyped by many as a non-caring, irresponsible group of people. This is very untrue! When health information is made available on a level that can be understood by average Americans, it makes a big difference. Some of this situation is changing because of creative methods that are used to reach minorities. Some venues used are churches, barber shops, and beauty parlors. Grants have been made available to provide free mammograms and other tests for early detection of diseases. Major radio and television networks' public-service announcements relative to hypertension, directed to minorities in the 1970s, were extremely effective; such methods should continue.

The second most significant change that I have seen has been in the area of inventions and technology. Despite

153

popular references, everything wasn't really good about the "good old days." For example, there wasn't complete electrification of all homes. The beginning of electrification started with the establishment of the Tennessee Valley Authority in 1933. At that time, this country was in the depths of the Great Depression; therefore, many citizens could not pay for electricity for their homes.

It also was not unusual for some people to heat "smoothing irons" on charcoal buckets to use for ironing. Added to this woe, polyester fabric was unknown. Sheets, shirts—everything—had to be ironed. Washboards and "number-two" tin tubs were the clothes washers of that day. Today, we have clothes dryers that help to make laundry day simpler and faster. Many other inventions, too numerous to mention here, also have made our everyday lives much easier.

The electronic technology of today is mind-boggling. I don't understand any of it because I am the world's greatest technophobe. The first computer that I saw filled a room. Today, we have laptop computers, small desktop personal computers, and even handheld palm pilots. Even more astonishing, a large computer company is developing a computer that can be carried in a pocket. In addition, the first calculator that I used was not portable; it was about 36 by 36 inches. Today, I carry a calculator in my purse.

I am sure that most children of today can't conceive of a world without television. The first time I heard of the possibility of anything like a television was in the 1930s. Daddy came home one day with this exciting news. He had heard of an invention that was being developed, which was a box similar to a radio; in it, a person could not only hear people, as on a radio, but also could see them as far away as New York City. For many of us, this idea probably seemed to be impossible; yet television became a reality for many homes by 1950. Today, there are few homes without at least one television.

As an Afro-American, the most historical event of my lifetime has been the Civil Rights Movement, which united us as a race more than ever before. But there were still dissenters among us. Many older Blacks shook their heads when they saw our young people participating in peaceful demonstrations. They said, "They ought to be ashamed." I still remember, with pride, the elderly Black woman in Montgomery, Alabama, who was honoring the bus boycott by walking across town to her job as a domestic worker. A young Black man saw her and told her that she didn't have to walk. She replied, "I am not walking for myself; I am walking for my grandchildren." I also remember an elderly White woman who sincerely could not understand why Blacks were demonstrating. She said in total dismay, "But we thought the Coloreds were happy." These were two completely different perceptions of race relations in the South at that time. They confirm Paul Lawrence Dunbar's assertion that "We wear the mask that grins and lies."

Many good things came out of the Civil Rights Movement. One important achievement was the right to vote. My mother was 63 years old when she was able to vote for the first time, for President Kennedy. She wrote a letter to me expressing her pride at having this right at last. As an American, in her memory and in memory of those who fought and died for us to have that right, I never miss an opportunity to vote. I can't understand people who don't vote and say, "My vote won't count, anyway." If our votes don't count, why are there those who still don't want us to vote? I believe that those who don't vote have no right to complain about what goes on in this country.

I also was happy to see affirmative action take place. I thought that now that we are given opportunities for better jobs and better education, Whites could see that there are truly qualified Afro-Americans. As a result, we moved ahead for a short time. In recent years, though, attempts have been made to dismantle affirmative action and other gains from the Civil Rights Movement. With these gains, we really thought our time had come. Perhaps we are like the frog in the African proverb that says, "Although I have nothing, I will always have my hope." But we aren't frogs; we can do better than just hope. We need to remember history because those who don't remember history will repeat the past. A good example of this is the hope that we had during the Reconstruction period. Former slaves held high government offices, and the future looked good for us. We had hope that our time had come, but, as W.E.B. Du Bois said then, "We stood in the sun for one brief moment." We had that same hope with the advances that we made as a result of the Civil Rights Movement. Some of those gains have been eroded; therefore, the Movement isn't over.

Along with the gains that we made from the Civil Rights Movement, some Blacks have been able to move ahead while others have been left behind. As a result, a class struggle has developed that has fragmented the Black community. Some Afro-Americans are so caught up in keeping each other down that we have lost sight of what we can do to help all Blacks. This circumstance has divided us as a race, just as color of complexion divided us for years. Using class exclusively to determine that some Blacks are better than other Blacks is no different than using color of complexion as a determinant. Both of these attitudes can be characterized as a "slave mentality." We have to remember that it doesn't matter what our accomplishments are in this country; we are still Black, and all of us are judged by the same stereotype and all that it implies. As one of our Civil Rights leaders said, "The only justification for looking down on somebody is to pick them up."

We can do some things for ourselves that would give us a better life, no matter what our race but especially as Afro-Americans. One thing that each race should do is to unite as a race. However, I can think of no other ethnic group in this country that is as divided as the Afro-American. Unity would make us strong! We need to nullify the statement that was made by Henry Baker, an 83-year-old former slave who was interviewed in Alabama in 1938. He said, "Blacks will never unite to accomplish anything." The scriptures (Ecclesiastes 4:12 NLT) say, "A person standing alone can be attacked and defeated, but two can stand back to back and conquer. Three are even better, for a triple-braided cord is not easily broken." I don't believe that we will be free as a race until we come together as a strong unit, a powerful force.

The quest for education and knowledge is still as important for us today in an effort to get ahead as it has ever been. It has been said, "What I know that you ought to know but do not know makes me powerful." There is no excuse for our not being an informed people. Unlike many of our ancestors, we have free education for our children through the high-school level and public libraries with free access to books; yet there are parents who are not concerned about their children's school attendance. They should remember that our ancestors weren't allowed to learn to read. In fact, we weren't even allowed to use the public library at the time and place where I grew up. I am glad to say, though, that many Afro-Americans, realizing that some of our children grow up in homes where there is no direction or stimulus, have become tutors and mentors. We need more of us to provide these types of activities for our children.

At this time in my life, I realize that I have more yesterdays than tomorrows. It is only normal to think of my mortality and how I wish to be remembered. I have wanted to be judged only by the content of my character, not by how many degrees I have or by the positions I have held in my life. Character is how God and the angels know me. Reputation is what people say about me.

Pride is included as one of the seven deadly sins in the Bible. However, I agree with the writer Michael Dyson when he says, "Pride is a virtue if it's pride in one's own heritage. Pride becomes a sin when it is used as prejudice against other people's beliefs and cultures." I am proud of the strength of my ancestors, who survived the slave ship and endured slavery. That strength is in all of us, and we need to continue to use it in ways to become a strong people.

I am proud of the life lessons that my parents taught to my brother and me. I am also proud of my three sons (one deceased), who grew up to be decent and honorable. Each is a college graduate, and one has a Ph.D. I also am proud of my seven grand-children. Four are college graduates, and one is an attorney. The other three, one of whom is a police officer, are hard-working, contributing members of society. As I look back over my life, I realize that it has been hard, but it has also been good. I am truly proud to be proud.

BIBLIOGRAPHY

Black Southerners 1610-1869
By John B. Boles
Copyright 1984. Lexington KY: University Press of
Kentucky, Lexington, KY

*Reconstruction and Reaction – The Emancipation of
Slaves 1861-1913*
By Michael Golay
Copyright 1996. Facts on File, New York, NY

Black Culture and the Harlem Renaissance
By Cory D. Wintz
Copyright 1988. A&M University Press, College
Station, TX

Slave Testimony
Edited by John W. Blassingame
Copyright 1977. Louisiana State University Press,
Baton Rouge, LA

The Creek Indian
By Evelyn Scordato
Copyright 1993. Chelsa House Publishing Co., New
York, NY

Black Reconstruction in America, 1860-1880
By W.E.B. Du Bois
Copyright 1992. Atheneum, New York, NY

Emancipating Slaves, Enslaving Free Men
By Jeffery Rogers Hummel
Copyright 1996. Open Court, Chicago, IL

Black Indian Geneology Research
By Angela Y. Walton-Raji
Copyright 1993. Heritage Books, Inc., Bowie, MD

Fighting in the Jim Crow Army – Black Men and Women Remember World War II
By Maggie M. Morehouse
Copyright 2000. Rowan and Littlefield Publishers, Lanham, MD

Booker T. Washington –
The Wizard of Tuskegee, 1901-1915
By Louis R. Harlan
Copyright 1983. Oxford University Press, Oxford and New York

Red-Tail Angels – The Story of the Tuskegee Airmen of World War II
By Patricia and Frederick McKissach
Copyright 1995. Walker and Company, New York, NY

Booker T. Washington 1856-1915, Up From Slavery with Introduction by Ishmael Reed
Copyright 2000. New America Library, New York, NY

About the Author

Mary Dillingham is an 80 year old Afro-American who grew up in the small Alabama town of Anniston. Her father was a Baptist minister and her mother a teacher. She is the grandaughter of former slaves. A graduate of Tuskegee Institute (Tuskegee University), she holds a Masters degree from Ohio State University. A dietetic internship was completed at Beth Israel (Beth Israel Deaconess) hospital in Boston, Massachusetts. She retired after a long career as a registered dietitian and teacher.

Made in the USA
Middletown, DE
20 November 2022

15619186R00099